■ THE NEW IMMIGRANTS ■

Filipino Americans

Indian Americans

Jamaican Americans

Korean Americans

Mexican Americans

Ukrainian Americans

Vietnamese Americans

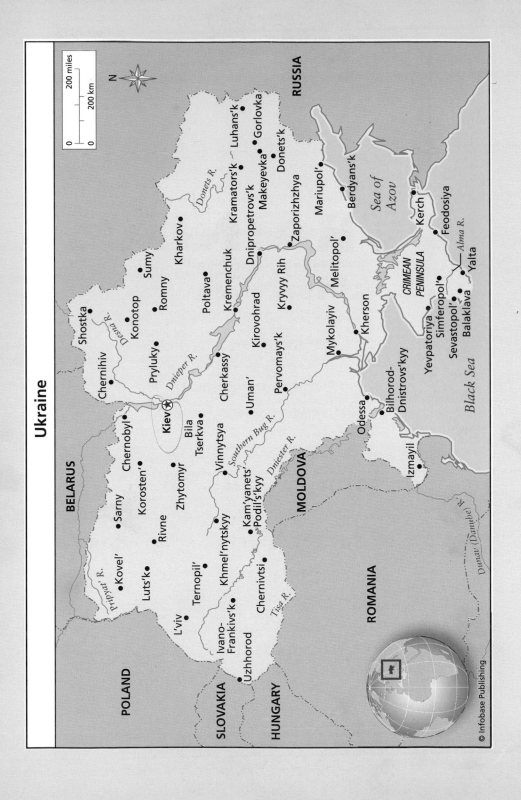

Ukraine

■ THE NEW IMMIGRANTS ■

UKRAINIAN
AMERICANS

John Radzilowski

Series Editor: Robert D. Johnston
Associate Professor of History,
University of Illinois at Chicago

CHELSEA HOUSE
PUBLISHERS
An imprint of Infobase Publishing

Frontis: Located in eastern Europe, Ukraine is the continent's second-largest country. According to the 2000 U.S. census, 862,762 people of Ukrainian descent called the United States home.

Ukrainian Americans

Chelsea House
An imprint of Infobase Publishing
132 West 31st Street
New York NY 10001

Library of Congress Cataloging-in-Publication Data
Radzilowski, John, 1965–
  Ukrainian Americans / John Radzilowski.
     p. cm. — (The new immigrants)
  Includes bibliographical references and index.
  ISBN 0-7910-8789-1 (hardcover)
1. Ukrainian Americans—History—Juvenile literature. 2. Immigrants—Unit-ed States—History—Juvenile literature. 3. Ukraine—Emigration and immigra-tion—Juvenile literature. 4. United States—Emigration and immigration—Juvenile literature. I. Title. II. New immigrants (Chelsea House)
E184.U5R33 2006
973'.0491791—dc22   2006015644

Series design by Erika K. Arroyo
Cover design by Takeshi Takahashi

Printed in the United States of America
Bang EJB 10 9 8 7 6 5 4 3 2 1
This book is printed on acid-free paper.

Contents

	Introduction	6
1	Ukrainians in North America	11
2	Ukraine: Land of Promise and Tragedy	21
3	Coming to North America	37
4	Building a New World	53
5	Making a New Home	64
6	Bringing Ukrainian Traditions to North America	81
7	The Newest Ukrainians in North America	94
	Chronology	111
	Timeline	112
	Notes	115
	Glossary	116
	Bibliography	118
	Further Reading	119
	Index	121

Introduction

Robert D. Johnston

At the time of the publication of this series, there are few more pressing political issues in the country than immigration. Hundreds of thousands of immigrants are filling the streets of major U.S. cities to protect immigrant rights. And conflict in Congress has reached a boiling point, with members of the Senate and House fighting over the proper policy toward immigrants who have lived in the United States for years but who entered the country illegally.

Generally, Republicans and Democrats are split down partisan lines in a conflict of this sort. However, in this dispute, some otherwise conservative Republicans are taking a more liberal position on the immigration issue—precisely because of their own immigrant connections. For example, Pete Domenici, the longest-serving senator in the history of the state of New Mexico, recently told his colleagues about one of the most chilling days of his life.

In 1943, during World War II, the Federal Bureau of Investigation (FBI) set out to monitor U.S. citizens who had ties with Italy, Germany, and Japan. At the time, Domenici was 10 or 11 years old and living in Albuquerque, with his parents—Alda, the president of the local PTA, and Cherubino, an Italian-born grocer who already had become a U.S. citizen. Alda, who had arrived in the United States with her parents when she was three, thought she had her papers in order, but she found out otherwise when federal agents swept in and whisked her away—leaving young Pete in tears.

It turned out that Alda was an illegal immigrant. She was, however, clearly not a security threat, and the government released her on bond. Alda then quickly prepared the necessary paperwork and became a citizen. More than six decades later, her son decided to tell his influential colleagues Alda's story, because, he says, he wanted them to remember that "the sons and daughters of this century's illegal immigrants could end up in the Senate one day, too."[1]

Given the increasing ease of global travel, immigration is becoming a significant political issue throughout the world. Yet the United States remains in many ways the most receptive country toward immigrants that history has ever seen. The Statue of Liberty is still one of our nation's most important symbols.

A complex look at history, however, reveals that, despite the many success stories, there are many more sobering accounts like that of Pete Domenici. The United States has offered unparalleled opportunities to immigrants from Greece to Cuba, Thailand to Poland. Yet immigrants have consistently also suffered from persistent—and sometimes murderous—discrimination.

This series is designed to inform students of both the achievements and the hardships faced by some of the immigrant groups that have arrived in the United States since Congress passed the Immigration and Naturalization Services Act in 1965. The United States was built on the ingenuity and hard work of its nation's immigrants, and these new immigrants—primarily from Asia and Latin America—have, over the last several decades, added their unique attributes to American culture.

Immigrants from the following countries are featured in THE NEW IMMIGRANTS series: India, Jamaica, Korea, Mexico, the Philippines, Ukraine, and Vietnam. Each book focuses on the present-day life of these ethnic groups—and not just in the United States, but in Canada as well. The books explore their culture, their success in various occupations, the economic hardships they face, and their political struggles. Yet all the authors in the series recognize that we cannot understand any of these groups without also coming to terms with their history— a history that involves not just their time in the United States, but also the lasting legacy of their homelands.

Mexican immigrants, along with their relatives and allies, have been the driving force behind the recent public defense of immigrant rights. Michael Schroeder explains how distinctive the situation of Mexican immigrants is, particularly given the fluid border between the United States and its southern neighbor. Indeed, not only is the border difficult to defend, but some Mexicans (and scholars) see it as an artificial barrier—the result of nineteenth-century imperialist conquest.

Vietnam is perhaps the one country outside of Mexico with the most visible recent connection to the history of the United States. One of the most significant consequences of our tragic war there was a flood of immigrants, most of whom had backed the losing side. Liz Sonneborn demonstrates how the historic conflicts over Communism in the Vietnamese homeland continue to play a role in the United States, more than three decades after the end of the "American" war.

In turn, Filipinos have also been forced out of their native land, but for them economic distress has been the primary cause. Jon Sterngass points out how immigration from the Philippines—as is the case with many Asian countries—reaches back much further in American history than is generally known, with the search for jobs a constant factor.

Koreans who have come to this country also demonstrate just how connected recent immigrants are to their "homelands" while forging a permanent new life in the United States. As Anne Soon Choi reveals, the history of twentieth-century Korea—due to Japanese occupation, division of the country after World War II, and the troubling power of dictators for much of postwar history—has played a crucial role in shaping the culture of Korean Americans.

South Asians are, arguably, the greatest source of change in immigration to the United States since 1965. Padma Rangaswamy, an Indian-American scholar and activist, explores how the recent flow of Indians to this country has brought not only delicious food and colorful clothes, but also great technical expertise, as well as success in areas ranging from business to spelling bees.

Jamaican Americans are often best known for their music, as well as for other distinctive cultural traditions. Heather Horst and Andrew Garner show how these traditions can, in part, be traced to the complex and often bitter political rivalries within Jamaica—conflicts that continue to shape the lives of Jamaican immigrants.

Finally, the story of Ukrainian Americans helps us understand that even "white" immigrants suffered considerable hardship, and even discrimination in this land of opportunity. Still, the story that John Radzilowski portrays is largely one of achievement, particularly with the building of successful ethnic communities.

I would like to conclude by mentioning how proud I am to be the editor of this very important series. When I grew up in small-town Oregon during the 1970s, it was difficult to see that immigrants played much of a role in my "white bread" life. Even worse than that ignorance, however, were the lessons I learned from my relatives. They were, unfortunately, quite suspicious of all those they defined as "outsiders." Throughout his life my grandfather believed that, Japanese who immigrated to his rural valley in central Oregon were helping Japan during World War II by collecting scrap from gum wrappers to make weapons. My uncles, who were also fruit growers, were openly hostile toward the Mexican immigrants without whom they could not have harvested their apples and pears.

Fortunately, like so many other Americans, the great waves of immigration since 1965 have taught me to completely rethink my conception of America. I live in Chicago, a block from Devon Avenue, one of the primary magnets of Indian and Pakistani immigrations in this country (Padma Rangaswamy mentions Devon in her fine book in this series on Indian Americans). Conversely, when my family and I lived in Storm Lake, Iowa, in the early 1990s, immigrants from Laos, Mexico, and Somalia were also decisively reshaping the face of that small town. Throughout America, we live in a new country—one not without problems, but one that is incredibly exciting and vibrant. I hope that this series helps you appreciate even more one of the most special qualities of the American heritage.

Note

1. Rachel L. Swarns, "An Immigration Debate Framed by Family Ties," *New York Times,* April 4, 2006.

Robert D. Johnston
Chicago, Illinois
April 2006

1

Ukrainians in North America

Imagine you are walking down the street in any American or Canadian city. You pass a shop with unfamiliar Cyrillic lettering. From inside come intriguing, tantalizing smells. You step inside and see a white tile floor and glass cases all around.

On one side, there is a long case of meats. A pile of sausages labeled *kovbasa* gives off a smoky, garlicky smell. On the other side, a shop assistant is pulling warm loaves of dark rye bread from a tray and wrapping them for customers. In the middle, the shopkeeper is preparing lunch in anticipation of the coming noon hour. You see a kettle of dark red beet soup. A platter of dumplings filled with potato and cheese is labeled *varenyky*. Plump rolls made of cabbage leaves stuffed with rice and meat are nearby. Next to these are sweet breads and pastries with names like *babka* and *kolachi*.

The shopkeeper turns, and, seeing you there, smiles and says, "Dobry den! How can I help you?"

Where are you? There is only one place you can be: a Ukrainian deli! A shop like this can be found in nearly every Ukrainian community. It is a place to gather, share a meal (or perhaps a cup of tea and a slice of babka), and meet friends and neighbors.

Ukrainian immigrants and their children and grandchildren can be found throughtout North America, from big cities to farms and small towns. According to the 2000 U.S. census, 862,762 people claimed Ukrainian ancestry, while the 2001 Canadian census listed 1,071,060 residents with Ukrainian ancestry. These citizens work in wheat fields and skyscrapers, as well as in neighborhood delis. They share pride in their ancient heritage and in their newly independent homeland. Some Ukrainian families came to these shores generations ago, whereas others arrived in the past few years. Together, they make up the fabric of Ukrainian life in North America, adding their special contribution to the multicultural nations of the United States and Canada.

EARLY ROOTS

The first Ukrainians to arrive in North America may have come as early as the 1770s. Several individuals with Ukrainian-sounding names settled in Pennsylvania before the American Revolution. During the Civil War, General John Basil Turchin, whose Ukrainian name was Ivan Vasilevitch Turchininoff, served in the Union Army and won fame for his gallantry at the Battle of Chickamauga in Tennessee.

In 1865, Reverend Agapius Honcharenko arrived in the United States. In Europe, Reverend Honcharenko had criticized the Russian emperor who then ruled most of Ukraine. He had to escape to America to avoid being persecuted for his beliefs. In America, Reverend Honcharenko worked as a Greek-language teacher and an editor. At that time, the United States had just purchased Alaska from Russia and was looking for a way to communicate with the inhabitants of this vast new land.

In 1868, the U.S. government hired Reverend Honcharenko to found a newspaper titled the *Alaska Herald*. It was published in Russian and English and later was independently owned by Reverend Honcharenko. He published information about the United States, selections from Ukrainian literature, and articles that promoted the rights of native Alaskans.

SURGING IMMIGRATION

The first large groups of immigrants from Ukraine came to the United States in the 1870s. They were called *Ruthenians* or *Carpatho-Rusyns* and lived in the Carpathian Mountains, a region that was then ruled by the Austro-Hungarian Empire. The exact

The Ruthenians were the first large group of people from Ukraine to immigrate to the United States when they left Ukraine in the 1870s. Composed of three groups—Lemkos, Hutsuls, and Bojkos—Ruthenians lived in the Carpathian Mountains of western Ukraine and were primarily shepherds and farmers. Pictured here are two Hutsul men and women dressed in traditional clothing.

number of these early immigrants is not known. Immigration statistics before 1899 often recorded these new arrivals as "Russian" or "Austrian," because Ukrainian lands were ruled by Russia and Austria at that time.

After 1899, about 250,000 Ukrainians entered the United States. Some of these immigrants came only as temporary workers and returned to Ukraine after a period of time, but many stayed to work in mines and factories and establish farms and communities.

The first Ukrainians to arrive in Canada were Wasyl Eleniak and Ivan Pylypiw, who landed in Montreal on September 7, 1891. Their enthusiastic reports about the large farms available in the western provinces convinced many other Ukrainians to follow in their footsteps. By 1914, about 100,000 Ukrainians had settled in Canada.

Another wave of Ukrainians came to North America in the 1920s, after World War I and the Russian Revolution. Even more Ukrainians arrived after World War II. Most were refugees fleeing war and devastation in Europe. A small number of Ukrainians came in the period from 1954 to 1991. In 1991, after Ukraine declared its independence, Ukrainians had more

Ukrainian Immigration to Canada	
Year of Entry	**Number Admitted**
1891–1914	100,000
1922–1929	70,000
1945–1954	32,000
1955–1960	4,500
1961–1991	5,600
1992–2000	20,000

* These periods mark the time when the largest number of Ukrainian immigrants entered Canada.

Ukrainian Immigration to the United States	
Year of Entry	**Number Admitted**
1899–1914	254,376
1920–1939	40,000
1948–1952	85,000
1991–2004	200,000

* These periods mark the time when the largest number of Ukrainian immigrants entered the United States.

freedom to emigrate. Some came to the United States or Canada in search of work. Others came to join family that was already here. Today, there are about one million Ukrainian Americans and nearly 600,000 Ukrainian Canadians.

Ukrainian immigrants settled across all of North America. They can be found on farms on the Great Plains. They worked in mines and factories of the East and Midwest. They opened businesses, established churches, served in the armed forces, contributed to science and the arts, and built communities that are an important part of North America.

RISE FROM HUMBLE BEGINNINGS

One immigrant claimed that he came to North America with "nothing but my ten fingers," which was true of many of the first Ukrainian immigrants. The Ukrainian homeland was under Russian and Austrian rule, and most people had little opportunity to go to college. Without education and unable to speak English, Ukrainian immigrants were often given the most difficult and dangerous jobs. They worked in factories and coal mines, where the accident rate was often very high and the hard work was exhausting. Many in Canadian and American society looked down on Ukrainians and other new

(continues on page 18)

FAMOUS UKRAINIAN AMERICANS AND UKRAINIAN CANADIANS

ALEXANDER ARCHIPENKO (1887–1964)

By the time he immigrated to the United States in 1923, Alexander Archipenko was on his way to becoming a world-famous painter and sculptor. Born in Ukraine in 1887, he spent several years in Paris, where he was influenced by the works of Pablo Picasso. While in Europe, he had numerous exhibits and even opened two art schools. His work bridged many styles, from abstract expressionism to cubism. After World War II, Archipenko created the concept of "modeling light" that makes space itself a form of sculpture.

ROBERTA BONDAR (1945–)

In 1992, Roberta Bondar joined the crew of the U.S. Space Shuttle *Discovery* and became the first Canadian woman in space. An eminent scientist who specialized in agriculture, zoology, neurology, and space medicine, she has received 24 honorary degrees from universities around the world. She is also a well-known photographer whose work has documented the natural beauty of Canada. In 2003, Dr. Bondar became chancellor of Trent University, in Peterborough, Ontario. She has been named to the Women's Forum Hall of Fame, named one of Canada's top explorers, and honored with a Canadian postage stamp.

RAMON HNATYSHYN (1934–2002)

The son of Ukrainian immigrants to Canada, Ramon Hnatyshyn served as Canada's governor general (the official representative of Queen Elizabeth II and the highest-ranking official in Canada) from 1990 to 1995. He was the first Ukrainian Canadian to hold such a high government office. He brought his signature openness and friendly smile to the office, insisting that people call him Ray and reopening the historic grounds of the governor's mansion to the public. During his time as governor general, he created the Governor General's Performing Arts Awards, the Fight for Freedom Literacy Award, the Canadian Bar Association's Hnatyshyn Award, and scholarships in environmental engineering and science. He also served as Canada's justice minister. In that office, he successfully introduced legislation that dealt with child abuse, gave police the right to seize the proceeds of suspected crimes, gave judges the power to order convicted criminals to compensate their victims, and enabled suspected Nazi war criminals to be tried in Canada. Despite his many honors, Hnatyshyn never forgot his Ukrainian heritage and was active in Ukrainian organizations throughout his life.

JACK PALANCE (1919–)

Perhaps the most famous North American actor of Ukrainian descent, Jack Palance was born Vladimir Palahniuk in Lattimer, Pennsylvania, the son of a Ukrainian immigrant miner. After serving in the U.S. Army and becoming a professional boxer, Palance pursued a career in acting. His film debut was in *Panic in the Streets* (1950), and he then went on to star in numerous films. He specialized in cowboy movies and films in which his rugged features helped him land "tough guy" roles. In addition to feature films, he starred in Broadway plays and on several television shows. He was twice nominated for Best Supporting Actor—in 1952 for *Sudden Fear* and in 1953 for *Shane*—but he didn't win an Oscar until 1992, when he was named Best Supporting Actor in the comedy *City Slickers*.

TERRY SAWCHUK (1929–1970)

Terry Sawchuk was one of the greatest goalies in professional hockey history. Born in Winnipeg, Manitoba, Sawchuk lost his brother to a heart ailment when he was 10 years old. Sawchuk won Rookie of the Year honors in the United States Hockey League and American Hockey League before landing with the Detroit Red

(continues on page 18)

(continued)

Wings of the NHL in 1950. He continued his superb play by recording a 1.99 goals-against average in his NHL rookie year, appearing in the All-Star Game and winning the Calder Memorial Trophy as the league's best first-year player. He was an All Star in the next four seasons and won three Vezina Trophies. Terry Sawchuck was a true reflex goalie. He did not pay as much attention to angles and technique, instead focusing on his quickness and explosive movement within the crease. During his 21-year NHL career, he played with the Los Angeles Kings, Detroit Red Wings, Boston Bruins, and New York Rangers. He finished with a record 447 wins and 103 shutouts and was inducted into the Hockey Hall of Fame in 1971.

WILLIAM TERON (1932–)

Outstanding North American businessman and architect William Teron began his career in 1951 as an architectural designer and in 1955 established a company to design and build real estate developments. Over the next 18 years, the Teron organization designed and built thousands of housing units, many hotels, office buildings, and shopping centers. His best-known work is the new town of Kanata, which is just outside Ottawa and referred to as Canada's Silicon Valley. Teron assembled and bought the land, planned the town as a "garden city," and built homes, industrial high-tech buildings, and community facilities. Teron's companies have built more than 4-million-square feet of buildings in Canada, the United States, and Europe.

(continued from page 15)

immigrants as inferior. They were often treated as second-class citizens.

Ukrainians had a tremendous will to endure such hardships and an unshakable desire to build a better life for their children. Through their hardships, they pulled themselves up by their bootstraps in the hope that their children and grandchildren would have new opportunities that they themselves would not enjoy. They believed in the promises of freedom and equal rights offered by their new homelands, even when some in those societies would have denied such rights and freedoms to their new Ukrainian neighbors.

At the same time, Ukrainians in North America did not forget their homeland. Ukraine did not enjoy independence until 1991. Before then, it was frequently invaded and fought over. It was also subject to harsh and terrible dictatorial rule

Ukrainian immigrants settled throughout the United States and established churches in many cities, including Pittsburgh, Pennsylvania. Pictured here is St. John the Baptist Ukrainian Catholic Church, which was built in 1895 and is considered the oldest Catholic church of the Byzantine Rite in the United States.

during the Soviet period of 1918 to 1990. During these years, many Ukrainians had to flee their homes. Some came to North America to escape persecution. Ukrainian communities in the United States and Canada worked hard to send help to their fellow Ukrainians in Europe. They raised money and supplies and used their new opportunity to vote to urge political leaders in the United States and Canada to act on Ukraine's behalf. When Ukraine gained independence in 1991, many Ukrainian Americans and Ukrainian Canadians helped their ancestral homeland toward a better future.

Along the way, Ukrainian immigrants and their children and grandchildren became a vital part of Canadian and American society. They became citizens and helped build farms and industry. They enriched the culture of both countries with new ideas, music, art, dance, and food. Over the years, as Ukrainians have continued to arrive in the New World, this history has been repeated. Without losing touch with their roots, Ukrainians in North America continue to play an important part in the future of Canada and the United States.

• Study Questions •

1. Who were some of the first Ukrainians in North America?
....

2. How many people of Ukrainian descent are there in North America?
....

2

Ukraine: Land of Promise and Tragedy

LAND AND PEOPLE

Ukraine is located in eastern Europe, just north of the Black Sea. It borders Russia on the east, Poland and Romania in the west, and Belarus in the north. Ukraine is the second-largest country in Europe. It is slightly smaller than the state of Texas or the province of Manitoba. Kiev, the capital of Ukraine, is located in the middle of the country.

Much of Ukraine is flat, fertile plains. Ukraine's thick topsoil makes it one of the best farming regions in Europe, and it has long been known as the "breadbasket" of eastern Europe. Southern Ukraine and the Crimean Peninsula are warm, sunny areas where grapes and fruit have been cultivated for centuries. The northern areas are cold and snowy in the winter and hot in the summer. The eastern section of Ukraine is known as the *Donbas* and is rich in natural resources such as coal and iron ore.

Ukraine is home to approximately 47 million people. Most Ukrainians speak the Ukrainian language. Ukrainian is a *Slavic* language related to Russian, Czech, and Polish. Most Ukrainians also speak Russian. In some areas of eastern Ukraine, the people speak only Russian. In addition to Ukrainians, Ukraine is home to many other peoples. Many Russians live in eastern and central Ukraine. In the south, Tatars live in the Crimea. Polish people live in the western areas of Ukraine, and Jewish Ukrainians can be found throughout the country. In the mountainous areas of western Ukraine live the Carpatho-Rusyns, a Slavic people closely related to Ukrainians.

EARLY HISTORY

Ukraine's flat, fertile fields have made it a kind of highway for people traveling from Asia to Europe. Over the centuries, many different nomadic people traveled across Ukraine. Some stayed, and others moved farther west. These ancient people were skilled hunters who knew how to survive Ukraine's harsh winters. Archeologists have discovered the oldest home ever made in Ukraine, a shelter made from the bones and hides of woolly mammoths. Later, Ukraine was home to many tribes of nomadic horsemen. The most famous were the Scythians.

During ancient times, Greek merchants founded cities along the Black Sea coast of Ukraine to trade with the Scythians and other people in the region. The Greeks brought grapes and made wine. Today, many areas of the Crimea still make wine.

The ancestors of Ukrainians were part of the Slavic group. The Slavs resided in central Asia and spoke a common language. About 2,000 years ago, the Slavic people left home and migrated west to settle in Ukraine and other parts of eastern and central Europe. About 1,500 years ago, the Slavs divided into many different tribes and groups. One of these groups became known as Ukrainians.

The first princes of Ukraine were Viking warriors from Scandinavia in the ninth century A.D. These warriors married

Slavic women and soon learned their language and culture. They began to unite many tribes in the region into a powerful force. Together, this small group of Vikings joined with the Slavic people of Ukraine to establish the first independent kingdom, called *Kievan Rus*. Its capital was Kiev, located on the Dnieper River. Kiev has remained the capital of Ukraine to this day.

The first ruler whose name is recorded by chronicles was Vladimir I, who ruled from approximately 980 to 1015. After Vladimir came Yaroslav the Wise (1019–1054), who wrote the first-known code of laws for Ukraine. He ruled Kiev with the help of powerful nobles (*boyars*) and an assembly of free farmers and townsfolk.

The people of Kievan Rus were powerful warriors but also skillful merchants and craftsmen. They traded with many other countries, including the mighty Byzantine Empire. This empire was a major center of eastern Christianity. In the year 988, the rulers and people of Kievan Rus converted to Christianity thanks to the influence of the Byzantines.

Under its ruling princes, the city of Kiev became rich and famous. During this period, it was known as the "Gold-Domed" city for its many churches, whose gold-colored domes reflected the sunlight and dazzled travelers. Mighty rulers such as Yaroslav the Wise built churches and monasteries. In addition to Kiev, many smaller cities also flourished under local princes.

In the year 1239, however, disaster fell on Ukraine. The Mongol hordes of Batu Khan turned their eyes to the riches of Ukraine. If they conquered Ukraine, they could also attack Europe. The Mongol armies attacked in the winter. The people of Kiev put up a valiant fight but the Mongols stormed the great city. They burned Kiev and killed many of its people; others were sold into slavery. For more than 100 years, Ukraine was under the harsh rule of the Golden Horde.

Kiev is sometimes referred to as the "Gold-Domed" city due to its large number of Orthodox churches with gold-colored domes. Pictured here is Pecherska Lavra Monastery, or the Kiev Monastery of the Caves, which was founded in the mid-eleventh century and today serves as the residence of the head of the Ukrainian Orthodox Church.

LITHUANIAN AND POLISH RULE

In the 1300s, the power of the Golden Horde began to wane. In the west, two rising powers began to challenge Mongol control. The first was the Lithuanians, distant cousins to the Slavic Ukrainians. The other was the Kingdom of Poland. The Poles were fellow Slavs but belonged to the Roman Catholic Church instead of the Orthodox Church familiar to most Ukrainians. In 1362, the Lithuanians smashed Mongol forces at the decisive Battle of Blue Waters. Much of western and central Ukraine fell under Lithuanian influence. The western region of Lviv, however, became part of the Kingdom of Poland in 1341. Faced with strong outside threats, these two countries joined together, forming a single powerful kingdom. They pushed the Tatars, descendents of the Mongols, back to the Crimea. Ukraine again knew peace.

Under Polish-Lithuanian rule, the local Ukrainians were able to govern themselves, and Ukrainian princes and nobles had the right to elect deputies to the country's parliament. The life of ordinary Ukrainian peasants who farmed the land changed little, however: Most remained poor. Some Ukrainians felt that they were second-class citizens in Poland, because Catholics sometimes looked down on Orthodox believers. In 1596, a large group of Orthodox Ukrainians joined the Catholic Church. This caused disputes to break out over religion, because people were divided on the issue of whether it was right to join the more unified Catholic Church of the West or remain under the looser authority of the Orthodox Church.

In the 1500s, the Polish kings and the parliament encouraged *Cossacks* to protect the Ukrainian border with the Crimea. Cossacks were free warriors. Some were former peasants who escaped to the borderlands seeking freedom. Others were impoverished nobles seeking to make their fortune on booty. They came from Ukraine but also from other countries. Together, they forged a powerful brotherhood of warriors. Fiercely independent, they kept invaders from raiding Ukraine and Poland—yet many felt that they were not well rewarded for their services. They wanted more political rights, such as the right to vote, and resented the power of Polish nobles whose clout was increasing in Ukraine.

In 1654, led by Bohdan Khmelnytsky, the Cossacks rose up in a great rebellion. Many peasants joined the rebellion. The rebels massacred many Poles and Jews whom they considered exploiters. Khmelnytsky's revolt weakened Poland but failed to help the Ukrainian people. Ukraine now fell under the power of a new neighbor: Russia.

UNDER THE RUSSIAN TSAR AND
THE AUSTRIAN EMPEROR

Russia gained control over Ukraine in the 1700s, and its influence was cemented in 1709, when Russian armies under Peter the Great defeated a Swedish invasion of east-central Europe at the Battle of Poltava. Western parts of Ukraine fell under the rule of the Austro-Hungarian Empire.

Russian rule was far harsher than Polish rule. The Russian tsar (emperor) sought to crush all ideas of independence. Ukrainians who disagreed were put in prison or sent to Siberia, where they had to perform hard labor. The life of ordinary Ukrainians was little different than that of slaves. Ukrainians who had joined the Catholic Church suffered special persecution. Jews in Ukraine were also treated harshly, and their right to move freely was restricted. The Ukrainian language was often replaced with Russian in the government and even in churches.

In western Ukraine, Austrian rule was slightly better. There, Ukrainians had a few rights and were not persecuted for religious reasons. The Ukrainian Catholic Church was able to exist without repression. Still, Ukrainians in Austria remained desperately poor.

Despite the repression suffered by Ukrainians, new ideas about freedom and justice began to spread. Educated Ukrainians began to work on behalf of the peasants. During this time, the first great poet of the Ukrainian language arose. He was Taras Shevchenko (1814–1861). Born a virtual slave, young Taras showed a talent for learning and was later set free. He composed epic poems that expressed the hopes for freedom and independence of the Ukrainian people. He used the language of the regular people of Ukraine and drew on their folk tales, songs, and history. Under Shevchenko's influence, new cultural and political movements arose. In many cases, Ukrainians formed secret societies (*hromada*) to teach their culture and spread the dream of a free Ukraine. Shevchenko helped inspire another important writer, Ivan Franko (1857–1916). Franko's poems and stories encouraged many Ukrainians to dream of a free Ukraine. As a result, the poet was often in trouble with the authorities.

It was during this period of Ukraine's history that many Ukrainians began to immigrate to North America in search of new opportunities. "America fever" began in the Austrian-controlled regions and later spread to the Russian-controlled areas. In North America, Ukrainians would have the opportunity to be free and make a better life for their children. Tens of thousands left, and in the years that followed, they were joined by family, friends, and neighbors.

DASHED HOPES

At the end of World War I, Communist revolutionaries led by V.I. Lenin overthrew the Russian tsar and established the Soviet Union. At first, the Soviet government promised independence for all peoples who had been denied their freedom by the tsar. Ukraine was rich in resources, however, and the Communists desired to possess it. In the west, Poland had regained its independence as well.

Many Ukrainians wanted to establish their own independent country, but they were caught between Poland and the Soviet Union. The Soviets also wanted to destroy Poland, and war broke out. The two sides fought over Ukraine. Lenin's effort to conquer Poland failed, but the peace agreement between the two sides partitioned Ukraine between them. Ukrainians in western Ukraine became part of Poland. The center of the country, including the capital, and the eastern regions became part of the Soviet Union.

With their hopes for independence dashed and their country wrecked by war, many Ukrainians immigrated to Canada or the United States. They were joined by immigrants from smaller Ukrainian communities in Czechoslovakia, Germany, and elsewhere.

THE FIRST SOVIET PERIOD, 1919–1939

Ukrainians who lived in Poland were often treated as second-class citizens, but those who lived in the Soviet Union suffered a good deal more. The Soviet government was a dictatorship far worse than that of the tsar. After the death of Lenin in 1924, Joseph Stalin became ruler of the Soviet Union. Stalin was determined to crush the Ukrainians so that Ukraine would always remain part of the Soviet Union.

Stalin's police and soldiers unleashed a reign of terror on Ukraine. Community leaders were arrested, tortured, and killed or sent to prison camps. Prosperous peasants were killed and their farms taken by the government. Beginning in 1931, the Soviet government took most of Ukraine's crops and food, leaving the people to starve. Millions of Ukrainians died in the Soviet Terror-Famine.

Ukrainian culture was also attacked. The Soviets tried to replace the Ukrainian language with Russian. Anyone who sought a free Ukraine could be arrested and imprisoned. Throughout the 1930s, Ukrainians suffered under a regime of tyranny.

WORLD WAR II

In 1939, Stalin joined Adolf Hitler, the dictator of Nazi Germany, in an alliance. Together, they attacked Poland and started World War II. For helping Hitler, Stalin received the western part of Ukraine, which had been under Polish rule. The Soviets encouraged conflict among the Ukrainians, the Poles, and the Jews in that territory. By encouraging people of different languages and religions to hate each other, they could take control more easily. During this period, Ukrainian Catholics in particular suffered greatly. The Soviets viewed the Ukrainian Catholic Church as a threat to their total control. Many churches were closed, and believers faced deportation to Siberia.

During the Soviet-implemented Terror-Famine of 1932–1933, millions of Ukrainians starved to death. The Terror-Famine is the largest national catastrophe in Ukraine's history and is also known as the *Holodomor*, which in Ukrainian means "to inflict death by hunger." Pictured here is a Ukrainian man holding a photo of his father during a commemorative rally in Kiev in 2005.

In June 1941, Hitler betrayed Stalin and attacked the Soviet Union. German armies quickly captured much of Ukraine, including Kiev. At first, many Ukrainians welcomed the invaders as liberators from the terrible regime of Stalin. Some Ukrainians even joined Hitler's armies. The Nazis encouraged Ukrainians to turn on Jews and Poles. As a result of the severe repression Ukrainians had endured, there was a rise of extremist Ukrainian

THE TERROR-FAMINE

The most tragic event in Ukrainian history is the *Holodomor*, or Terror-Famine, of 1932–1933. During these years, the Soviet government, led by Joseph Stalin, tried to destroy the Ukrainian people. Stalin's method was to take the food of Ukrainian farmers so that the people would starve.

The Soviet government wanted to control all Ukrainian land, and Stalin wanted all farming done collectively. That meant that the government would make all decisions about farming. The Ukrainian farmers, however, did not want to give up their small farms. Their way of farming produced more food than the Soviet way. They wanted to make their own decisions and not be controlled by the government.

The independent attitude of the Ukrainians enraged Stalin. He ordered his army and secret police to take the crops and animals from Ukraine. Food was taken from the people by force and stored under armed guard. Some people tried to fight the Soviet army with pitchforks. Those who resisted were killed or sent to labor camps.

While the warehouses bulged with food, the Ukrainians starved. Within three years, 3 to 4 million people died in Ukraine because of starvation or execution. As this was going on, Stalin was selling grain from Ukraine to other countries.

Soviet leaders looked on with indifference as people perished. They made a special effort to hide what was happening from the rest of the world and sent false reports that everything was fine. Those who tried to tell the truth were called liars and enemies of the Soviet people. Some newspaper reporters from Europe and North America believed Stalin and wrote articles that supported the Soviet Union. Despite the cover-up by the Soviet government, some visitors noticed what was going on in Ukraine. Author and groups dedicated to driving out all people considered different or alien, especially Jews and Poles.

radio commentator Carveth Wells was traveling through Ukraine and noted the dire conditions within the country:

> The extraordinary thing was that the farther we penetrated into the Ukraine, which used to be the "Granary of Russia," the less food there was and the more starvation to be seen on every side. . . . We ourselves happened to be passing through the Ukraine and the Caucasus in the very midst of the famine in July, 1932. From the train windows children could be seen eating grass.*

Ukrainian immigrants who lived in other countries tried to inform the world about this terrible event for a long time. Only since the collapse of the Soviet Union in 1989 has the world slowly come to recognize the full horrors of what happened to the Ukrainians under Soviet rule. One Ukrainian girl, Zina, recounted her situation to her uncle, shortly before she died of starvation:

> We have neither bread nor anything else to eat. Dad is completely exhausted from hunger and is lying on the bench, unable to get on his feet. Mother is blind from the hunger and cannot see in the least. So I have to guide her when she has to go outside. Please Uncle, do take me to Kharkiv, because I, too, will die from hunger. Please do take me, please. I'm still young and I want so much to live a while. Here I will surely die, for every one else is dying.**

---

* Carveth Wells, *Kapoot* (London: Jarrolds, 1933), 133. Available online at *http://209.82.14.226/history/famine/gregorovich/*

** Stephane Courtois, Nicholas Werth, Jean-Louis Panne, Andrzej Paczkowski, Karel Bartosek, and Jean-Louis Margolin, *Black Book of Communism* (Cambridge, Mass.: Harvard University Press, 1999). Available online at *http://www.faminegenocide.com/resources/genocide/index.html*

Ukrainians soon discovered that Germans were just as bad as the Soviets. Germans treated Ukrainians like slaves and sought to take the grain and other products of Ukraine for their own. Many Ukrainians perished because of repression and hunger during this period.

The Germans worked to kill all of Ukraine's Jews as part of their plan to destroy Jews everywhere, an event known as the Holocaust. Throughout the country, they tried to kill every Jewish man, woman, and child. Jewish synagogues, schools, and seminaries were burned, and the homes and businesses of Jews looted. The most infamous place was Babi Yar, a deep ravine where many of Kiev's Jews were shot to death. Some Ukrainians helped the Germans, but others risked their lives to save their Jewish neighbors. Among the most famous was the Ukrainian Catholic metropolitan of Lviv, Bishop Andrei Sheptytsky. Bishop Sheptytsky risked his life to protest the killing of Jews and helped hide hundreds of Jews during the war. In western Ukraine, Ukrainian extremists also targeted the Polish minority of that area, killing many and driving others from their homes.

After Germany's defeat, all of Ukraine again came under Stalin's rule. Many Ukrainians fled to Western Europe rather than endure life under the Soviet dictator. Some of these refugees made their way to North America to join fellow Ukrainians already there.

SOVIET RULE, 1945–1991

Soviet repression in Ukraine continued after the war. Many Ukrainians were uprooted from their homes and sent to Siberia or the barren regions of southern Russia. After the death of Stalin in 1956, conditions eased—but only a little. Most Ukrainians lived in fear, and only a few were able to leave their homeland for a better life in North America. Ukrainians in the United States and Canada kept the world informed about how the Soviets were treating Ukrainians.

In 1941, Nazi Germany invaded the Soviet Union and captured much of Ukraine. As they did throughout much of Europe during the Holocaust, the Nazis attempted to eradicate Ukraine's Jewish citizens. Pictured here is a monument at Babi Yar, where more than 30,000 Jews from Kiev were shot to death during a two-day period in September 1941.

In the 1980s, Soviet control began to weaken. In neighboring Poland, people began to defy the Soviet government. This spirit of independence began to spread to Ukraine. In 1986, a terrible accident occurred at the nuclear plant at *Chernobyl* in northern Ukraine. Many people died or were poisoned by radiation. Hundreds of thousands of people had to be evacuated from their homes. The Soviet authorities tried to cover up this accident, but soon people across Ukraine learned the truth from friends and neighbors. There was widespread outrage both in Ukraine and around the world.

Within a few years, the influence of the Soviet Union began to wane. In the late 1980s, Ukraine's neighbors to the west began their move toward freedom. The whole system of Soviet control began to falter. In 1991, the Soviet Union collapsed.

FROM INDEPENDENCE TO THE ORANGE REVOLUTION

On August 24, 1991, Ukraine declared itself an independent nation. For the first time in hundreds of years, there was again an independent Ukraine. People rejoiced in the streets. The gold and blue Ukrainian flag could be seen flying from buildings and homes.

For the first time, Ukrainians from the United States and Canada could visit their relatives in Ukraine freely and without fear. Many Ukrainians began to immigrate to the United States and Canada to reunite with families that had been divided by war and politics.

Ukraine also suffered many problems, however. The Communist Party of Ukraine kept much of the power. Former Soviet officials in Ukraine divided up the businesses, factories, and mines for themselves. The end of the Soviet Union left ordinary people in Ukraine very poor and without hope for jobs or a decent life. Many Russian people in eastern Ukraine did not want to speak Ukrainian and wanted Ukraine to once again be part of Russia.

During the first years of independence, life in Ukraine was difficult. Under the former Communists, the economy performed poorly and the government failed to enact the reforms needed to change the situation. President Leonid Kuchma controlled the country and began to act like a dictator. In 2004, a new election for president was to be held. Many Ukrainians placed their hopes in Victor Yushchenko, who promised reform, good government, and an end to the power of the old leadership. He was opposed by President Kuchma's handpicked candidate. The government controlled the media, including all the television stations. These television stations were used to try to make people distrust Yushchenko. When the results came in, it seemed as if Yushchenko had lost, but people soon found out that the election had been fixed. Kuchma's friends had falsified the results so that their side could win.

Many Ukrainians began to protest against the crooked election. On television, a brave sign-language interpreter, Natalia Dmytruk, defied the orders of her bosses and began to use sign language to inform the Ukrainian people that the election had been rigged. The protests grew and spread to almost every corner of Ukraine. Many of the protesters were students and young people who wore orange scarves and hats to show their support for reform. The Ukrainian government was paralyzed. Faced with peaceful protests for change, they finally agreed to a new election. The new vote would be watched by observers from other countries to make sure it was fair. .

In December 2004, the new election was held. Victor Yushchenko and his "orange" supporters won by a wide margin. The new government faced many problems, but it sought to solve them for the benefit of all Ukrainian people. For many Ukrainians, the peaceful *Orange Revolution* marked the true birth of a free Ukraine. It was an event many had hoped for all their lives.

• Study Questions •

1. Find Ukraine on a world map. Which countries are Ukraine's largest neighbors?
   ....

2. How did the Cossack brotherhood affect Ukraine's history?
   ....

3. Why did the Soviet Union seek to destroy Ukrainian culture?
   ....

4. What was the Terror-Famine?
   ....

3

Coming to North America

Getting to their new homes in North America was not always easy for Ukrainian immigrants. They faced many obstacles, two of which were poverty and lack of opportunity in their homeland that sometimes made it hard to pay for their travels. The journey itself was also hard and sometimes dangerous. Ukrainians had to endure loneliness and the pain of being separated from their family, friends, and homeland.

Each step of the journey brought new experiences for the immigrants; some were difficult, others joyful or fascinating. At each point in their journey, Ukrainians had to respond with creativity and perseverance.

VILLAGE AND FAMILY LIFE

Before coming to North America, most Ukrainians were peasants. Peasants were farmers whose rights and freedoms were often limited. As in many countries, peasant farmers in Ukraine

37

lived in villages. Villages ranged in size from a few families to as many as 1,000 or more inhabitants.

Larger villages had a market square, where farmers would gather to trade and sell their products or buy what they needed. Businesses and shops in many villages were owned by Jewish families who worked as middlemen, buying the farm goods from the peasants and taking them to larger towns to sell. Jewish merchants and craftsmen often sold, made, or repaired the few finished or imported goods that the peasants needed, including matches, sugar, tobacco, liquor, shoes, and cloth.

Another important part of the village was the church, and important towns sometimes had more than one (in addition to a Jewish synagogue). The church was the center of cultural life for the peasants. It gave them spiritual comfort in their often-difficult lives. Church feast days and holidays provided an opportunity for cultural expression, a chance to socialize with friends and neighbors, and a break from work. Priests were important leaders in the village, providing advice and help as well as moral guidance. They blessed the peasants' fields, animals, and homes and led the community in prayers for good harvests, mild weather, and protection against sickness or natural disaster.

The passing of each year in the life of the village was marked by a regular series of festivals and rituals that gave meaning and structure to the peasants. One special custom observed throughout Ukraine was the blessing of the water. Each January, after Christmas, the priest would lead the villagers to a local stream or river and break a small hole in the ice to bless the water in remembrance of Jesus's baptism. Peasants would splash a little water on themselves and then take some of the water in pails or bowls to be used for blessing the home and the farm animals.

Another popular custom was Christmas caroling. Young men would go through the village and sing songs. In return, villagers, especially wealthier ones, were expected to provide

Caroling is one of the most popular Christmas customs among Ukrainians. This 1860 rendition of a group of carolers, called *Christmas Carols in the Ukraine*, is by Konstantin Trutovsky and is on display at the State Russian Museum in St. Petersburg.

food and drink. One account recalled, "For the host it is a point of honor to organize hospitality on the most lavish scale to keep the goodwill of the volunteers." Wealthier members of the village were expected to be generous to the carolers to ensure that they kept a good reputation. In each village, especially in the mountains of western Ukraine, villagers formed companies (*kumpanii*) for caroling, each led by a head caroler. Known as the birch tree, the head caroler was chosen on the basis of his knowledge of carols and other songs and for his ability to make toasts that would honor the head of each household the carolers were to visit. The leader would often tailor the songs to fit each family they visited, uplifting the poorer members of the community and praising the generosity of the wealthier ones. Each company had a few musicians, such as a fiddler, and assigned one member to act as the "horse" to carry gifts received at each household.[1]

These celebrations helped enliven the lives of Ukrainian peasants, for their work was hard and unending. They worked from dawn to dusk every day, except Sunday and church holidays. In the summer, they worked outside in the broiling sun, cutting hay or grain. In the winter, they froze in Ukraine's icy cold weather. Their homes were small and modest, usually made of logs and covered with mud plaster. The floors were dirt, covered with straw or rushes, and roofs were made of thatch or tight bundles of grass. Food and fuel were often scarce, especially in the winter.

Droughts, floods, and sickness were feared by the peasants. Each of these could wreck their harvests and result in hunger during the coming year. Families kept a variety of animals—horses for work, cows for milk to make butter and cheese, chickens for eggs and meat, and pigs for meat. These animals were vital to the Ukrainian peasant: They often meant the difference between having enough to eat and going hungry. Because of this, peasants took special care of their animals. If a late spring snowstorm threatened newborn piglets or calves, peasant families might take the baby animals into their homes.

The family was the bedrock of Ukrainian life. It provided love and security and was vital to survive the hard living conditions peasants faced. Children were expected to work, even from a young age. Children as young as five or six would tend flocks of geese or help feed chickens or pigs. As they got older, they would be given more responsibility. Older children worked right alongside their parents—the boys with their fathers in the barns and fields and the girls with their mothers in the house and around the farm. Both men and women were essential to the family's survival. Each family member was vital, and the loss of one because of illness or to being drafted into the army was a serious blow.

Children were also expected to care for their parents in old age. There was no social security or pension plan, so families had to care for their own. Older boys might be sent out to work on a neighboring farm or girls to work as servants for wealthier families. The wages would help the family build a small retirement fund for the parents.

WHY DID THEY COME?

At the end of the nineteenth century, Ukrainian lands were the scene of great social and economic changes. For centuries, most Ukrainians had been subject to the system of serfdom. Under this system, Ukrainian peasants had little freedom. They had few chances to move or take a job other than farming and little opportunity to make a better life for themselves. Under serfdom, each peasant family was forced to provide the landlord or the government with a certain amount of farm produce, such as grain, milk, or eggs, or was required to work a certain number of days each month or year for the master. How much the family had to give or work each year varied from family to family and village to village. In return, peasants had the right to use a small amount of land, graze their animals in the village's pastures, collect a certain amount of wood from local forests, and use the village mill to grind their grain.

Serfdom was a very poor system of farming. In the late nineteenth century, governments sought a more modern system of farming that produced more food for expanding cities. Serfdom was eliminated and peasants gained freedom of movement. Instead of having to work for the government or their landlord, under the new laws peasants had to pay rent. They were now free from their old duties, but they had to come up with money. This was often very difficult for peasants. They had gained new freedom, but this freedom seemed to make them poorer.

Peasants sought to sell the products of their farms in the market place, but this did not bring in much money. Others hired themselves out to work for others—richer farmers, noblemen, or perhaps the government.

In many areas, peasants discovered that, by traveling to areas where workers were needed, they could earn higher wages. In some areas, very large farms that needed many workers were being created. In other places, there were new mines and factories looking for people to come and work. In these places, Ukrainian peasants could finally earn enough to pay their rents and perhaps a little bit extra. The extra money could be used to improve their farms or buy some extra food to make the winter months more pleasant.

These early migrants inspired others to think about traveling to earn money. The problem was that, in Ukraine and in neighboring countries, only a limited number of jobs were available. Because there were many former peasants looking for work, employers did not have to pay much to attract the laborers they needed.

The peasants began to hear of countries far away where wages were good, work was plentiful, and there was land for farming. These countries were the United States and Canada. Stories in newspapers and tales from early pioneers in these countries inspired many Ukrainians, especially young people, to dream of going to America. Only in America could peasants from simple villages earn enough money to make better lives for their families so that their children would no longer have to toil as they had toiled.

Mary Skoropat Hruby, daughter of Ukrainian immigrants to North Dakota, recalled her father's reason for emigrating: "Dad had a few acres. His idea was to come here, earn money, return to Ukraine and buy a farm. Five acres was a rich man in Ukraine."[2]

Speaking about his parents' decision to leave the village of Trubchyn, Peter Basaraba said, "There was 10 of us in the family and we had 24 morga—four and a half acres. Father thought to himself, when the kids take part of it, the kids won't have anything and I won't have anything. He sell out and came here."[3]

THE JOURNEY

Ukrainian immigrants tried to learn as much as they could before setting off on their journey to America. They talked to family and neighbors who had traveled beyond the village. They sought out articles in newspapers. (If they could not read, others might read the article to them.) Through letters, they also learned about what they would face from others who had traveled to the United States. Ukrainians might also learn about America from people of other ethnic groups who had family members in the United States. "When a letter came from America, whoever could read, read—and many came to listen,"[4] said Pearl Basaraba, whose parents eventually settled in North Dakota in 1906.

Many immigrants knew what part of North America they would go to. For example, many knew there were jobs to be had in the coal-mining region of Pennsylvania. If they had friends or relatives in America, they would write down that person's address on a piece of paper that they would take with them. Sometimes, their friends or relatives might send them a prepaid steamship ticket.

Leaving home was often the most difficult part of the journey. "The trains were filled with the weeping of people from the villages in *Galicia*, who were leaving their relatives, their birthplaces and their homes forever,"[5] remembered George Klym of his train ride from Lviv to the port city of Hamburg, Germany.

Because the journey was long and money was tight, Ukrainian immigrants would often bring as much food as they could, along with some extra clothing. Most took at least a little bit of money they had saved up or borrowed from others.

The first step was travel to a train station, usually by foot or, if the emigrant was lucky, by horse-drawn cart. This part could sometimes take days if the village was in a remote area. Once on the train, Ukrainian immigrants had to negotiate a new and unfamiliar world at each step of the way. The farther they got from home, the fewer people knew their language and the more they had to rely on one another and the assistance of friendly people they met along the way.

Their destination was one of the major ports in northern Germany, such as Bremen or Hamburg. These cities were brimming with immigrants from throughout Europe seeking to go to America aboard one of the steamships that sailed daily from these ports.

This part of the journey to the New World was exciting, confusing, and sometimes dangerous. For the first time, the immigrants were seeing new places. Cities were expanding and being transformed by new technology. The modern world opened up to the immigrants as they traveled. The journey was also confusing. There were new experiences, people speaking different languages, and many things to learn.

The journey to North America could also be dangerous. Many criminals preyed on immigrants. They knew that the immigrants were carrying money and tickets. Ukrainian villagers arriving in a big city like Bremen might seem lost and fearful, and it was easy for a criminal to pretend to be a helpful new friend while trying to swindle them. There were also kidnappers who looked for young women who seemed vulnerable or alone. Some immigrants disappeared, got lost, or were waylaid by criminals, and in many immigrant newspapers, worried families would take out classified ads seeking information about their missing loved ones.

From Bremen or Hamburg, most of the Ukrainian immigrants would board their ship for North America. Nearly all Ukrainians sailed in steerage, the lowest section of the ship in which passengers were allowed. The sea journey could also be difficult. Many immigrants had never been on the ocean and suffered seasickness. They also had to watch out for criminals who might be on board the ship.

In 1911, the U.S. government sent undercover investigators to check on the conditions for young women traveling from Europe on steamships. One investigator reported:

> One steward who had business in our compartment was as annoying a visitor as we had and he began his offenses soon after we left port. . . . Not one day passed but I saw him annoying some women, especially in the wash rooms . . . . The manner in which the sailors, stewards, firemen, and others mingled with the women passengers was thoroughly revolting. Their language and the topics of their conversations were vile. . . . The atmosphere was one of general lawlessness and total disrespect for women.[6]

Most Ukrainians who came during the first wave of Ukrainian immigration arrived at *Ellis Island* in New York City. As their ship approached the harbor, they would pass the Statue of Liberty. The first image of this monument to freedom was remembered by many Ukrainians their entire lives.

After disembarking at Ellis Island, the new arrivals would show their papers and have a brief interview with a customs agent. They would also be inspected for any known diseases. Once they had passed these tests, they were free to enter America and begin their new lives.

In the late 1920s and 1930s, immigration to North America declined among Ukrainians and most other groups from Europe. As a result, few newcomers came through Ellis Island. Ukraine had become part of the Soviet Union after World War I, and the new government refused to allow most Ukrainians the chance to go to North America. The conditions only got worse during World War II, when it was almost impossible to leave Europe. It wasn't until after the war ended that Ukrainians were able to immigrate to North America once again.

During the first wave of immigration to the United States, most Ukrainians passed through the main registry building on Ellis Island in New York Harbor, which is pictured here in 1905. Once these immigrants were legally and medically cleared to enter the United States, they were free to settle wherever they chose.

IMMIGRATION AFTER WORLD WAR II

During World War II, many Ukrainians fled their homes to escape war, hunger, and repression. Others were forced to become slave laborers for the Nazis. When the war ended, many Ukrainians were living in refugee camps in Germany and other countries.

The Soviet Union wanted these refugees to return, but many feared to go home. Years of living under Soviet repression had taught them that anyone who had lived in the West was a suspect in the eyes of the secret police. They did not believe Soviet promises. In some cases, British and American soldiers forced the refugees to return against their will. Those who did return often were arrested and sent to Siberia or mistreated by Soviet officials.

These refugees were people without a country. They were called *displaced persons,* or *DPs.* Because of the widespread destruction caused by the war, Ukrainian DPs, along with DPs of many nationalities, relied on assistance from the United Nations or from friends and compatriots who lived in North America. Most lived in refugee camps, where conditions were often difficult. Because of the problems caused by the war, many countries did not want to accept more immigrants.

In the early 1950s, however, the United States and Canada agreed to accept a large group of DPs, including many Ukrainians. This gave the displaced Ukrainians a chance for a new life and, if they were lucky, to reunite with family they had not seen in many years.

Like earlier Ukrainian immigrants, the DPs sailed to North America on ships, but after World War II, these ships often were U.S. Navy transport ships rather than ocean liners. These Ukrainian immigrants arrived at Ellis Island and were among some of the last immigrants to be processed there. Ellis Island closed in 1954.

THE NEWEST IMMIGRANTS

In recent years, Ukrainian immigrants who have come to the United States and Canada have used a more modern means of transportation: the airplane. Today, there are regular flights between Kiev and western Europe. Most immigrants fly from Kiev on a Ukrainian airline to Frankfurt, Germany, or Amsterdam, the Netherlands; then they catch a second flight to North America.

Immigrants seeking a new life must get a proper visa that will allow them to enter the United States or Canada. To do this, potential immigrants must fill out a visa application and send it to the American or Canadian embassy in Ukraine.

In the early 1950s, the United States and Canada agreed to accept many displaced persons, or DPs, after they fled the Soviet Union. Pictured here are a brother and sister who emigrated from Ukraine aboard the U.S. Navy transport *General Black* in 1950.

Ukrainians can come to the United States to join other family members who are already living there as citizens or legal immigrants. They may also come if offered jobs by American employers or if they marry American citizens. In addition, Ukrainians may apply for a visa under a special program where the U.S. government holds a lottery for potential immigrants from many countries. Those whose names are chosen may come to the United States.

Currently, to immigrate legally to the United States, Ukrainians must file a petition with the U.S. government (or have one filed for them by a friend or family member). Once the petitions have been approved, Ukrainians must apply for visas that will allow them to come to the United States. The most common type of immigrant from Ukraine is someone who has a family member in the United States and is coming to join that family member.

Immigrants to Canada may come if they help the country's economy, have relatives in Canada, or are victims of persecution in their homeland. Most immigrants to Canada from Ukraine come to join relatives or to work. Ukrainians who want to come to Canada must be in good health, be law-abiding, and have enough money to support themselves and their dependants during their stay. Just as in the United States, Ukrainians coming to Canada must first apply to the Canadian government and then get a visa that will allow them to come. Immigrants who plan to stay in Canada for more than six months may be required to undergo an immigration medical examination.

FINDING THEIR WAY

Whether they came to North America yesterday or came 100 years ago, the first step for Ukrainian immigrants was to find their way in new and unfamiliar circumstances. Early immigrants had the most difficult time, because there were few services to help them once they arrived.

UKRAINIANS AROUND THE WORLD

Canada and the United States are not the only countries where Ukrainian people live. Around the world, there are 5 to 10 million people of Ukrainian descent living outside of Ukraine. They reside on every inhabited continent. Many Ukrainians in North America have friends and relatives in these communities.

The largest group of Ukrainians living abroad is in Russia, where about 4 million reside. Because of centuries of Russian rule and because the Russian and Ukrainian languages are quite similar, many Ukrainians have migrated to Russia for work. Others have married Russians and live with their spouses. Over the centuries, Russian rulers also sought to resettle Ukrainian farmers in deserted areas of southern Russia and Siberia. About half of the Ukrainians in Russia live in the Kuban region, but Ukrainians can be found throughout Russia in both small towns and major cities like Moscow.

About 300,000 Ukrainians also live in neighboring Poland, especially in the southeastern part of the country. There are also Ukrainians living in southwestern Poland, where they were resettled during the Communist era. Along the Polish-Slovak border live the Carpatho-Rusyns, close cousins of the Ukrainians.

Ukrainian communities can also be found throughout Europe. Over the past 15 years, many Ukrainians have moved to countries in Europe to work. Some have done so for only a short period of time. They earn some money and then return to their families in Ukraine. Others have stayed longer and have started to put down

Many early immigrants came with only a piece of paper that showed the address and city in America where they wanted to go. If they could not find a friendly fellow Ukrainian who knew English, they would have to rely on the kindness of strangers. They would show the paper with the address to roots. Today, there are 200,000 Ukrainians working in Italy and 100,000 in Spain! Ukrainians can be found in nearly every country of the European Union.

Ukrainian immigrants can also be found in Argentina, Cyprus, Liberia, and the United Arab Emirates. Many Ukrainians live in Australia and New Zealand, as well.

COUNTRIES WITH LARGE UKRAINIAN POPULATIONS

Argentina and Brazil	400,000
Australia	40,000
Belarus	400,000
France	40,000
Germany	25,000
Great Britain	30,000
Italy	200,000
Kazakhstan	900,000
Kyrgyzstan	100,000
Moldova	600,000
Poland	300,000
Portugal	150,000
Romania	100,000
Russia	4,000,000
Slovakia	40,000
Spain	100,000
Uzbekistan	150,000

train conductors, ticket agents, or porters who would help them get on the right train at the right time. Once they arrived at their final stop, they would have to find the address of their friends or relatives, again relying on helpful people they met along the way.

More recent immigrants are able to contact their friends and relatives using phones or e-mail. There are also many agencies that will help immigrants find their way, interpret for them, and make sure that they don't get lost.

No matter when they come, when Ukrainian newcomers reach their destination, it is always with a sense of great relief, especially if they are reuniting with family and friends. Still, for the new arrivals, the immigrant journey is just beginning. Having arrived in North America, they must make this new place home.

• Study Questions •

1. What were some of the festivals that Ukrainian villagers celebrated?
   ....

2. How did families help Ukrainian peasants survive hard times?
   ....

3. Why did Ukrainians decide to immigrate to North America?
   ....

4. What challenges did Ukrainians have to overcome when they journeyed to America?
   ....

4

Building a New World

Once they arrived in North America, Ukrainian immigrants had to work hard to establish themselves. Most came to better their lives and the lives of their families and had known only poverty and lack of opportunity. Now they would have a chance to change that.

The first and most important step for the newly arrived Ukrainians has always been to find work. A job would provide security and a passport to a better life. Ukrainian immigrants have never been afraid to work hard, regardless of where or when they arrived in North America.

WHERE DID THEY SETTLE?

When the first Ukrainians came to the United States, many sought out jobs as coal miners. At first, a few Ukrainians from Austria-Hungary probably learned about mining jobs from Slovak, Hungarian, or Polish neighbors. Once a few Ukrainians had established themselves as miners, they told friends and relatives about the opportunities they had found. Because of this, some of the largest Ukrainian communities first emerged in the coal-mining regions of Pennsylvania. Towns like Shenandoah and Shamokin and cities like Pittsburgh and Scranton had strong Ukrainian communities by the 1880s. Ukrainians also found plenty of opportunity in the states of New York and New Jersey, where they often worked in the growing manufacturing and chemical industries.

In the Midwest, Ukrainian immigrants settled in South Chicago. They found jobs in meatpacking factories and steel mills. In Ohio and Michigan, they also worked in the steel and

After they immigrated to the United States, many Ukrainians tried their hand at coal mining and settled in the coal region of northeastern Pennsylvania. Today, many of these communities still have sizeable Ukrainian populations, especially around the town of Pottsville.

automotive industries. In Minnesota, Ukrainians found work in flour milling, railroads, and breweries.

Early Ukrainian immigrants in Canada looked for farmland and sought out homesteads on the western prairies in the provinces of Alberta, Saskatchewan, and Manitoba. Other immigrants found homes in Ontario in cities such as Toronto and Windsor.

Although most Ukrainian immigrants to North America settled in Ukrainian communities, many individuals traveled throughout the country to look for work or a place to call home. At least a few Ukrainians went to almost every state and province in North America, including Hawaii, Alaska, and the Yukon and Northwest Territories.

THE LIFE OF A COAL MINER

The earliest large Ukrainian communities formed in the coal country of Pennsylvania, where many Ukrainians found their first jobs as miners. Compared to wages in Ukraine, pay for a coal miner was good. During the 1890s and in the years that followed, coal mining in the United States was a vital industry. America's economy was expanding, and the fuel that made the country run was coal. Along with many other immigrant groups from central, eastern, and southern Europe, Ukrainians were a vital part of this great industrial growth.

This growth came with a price. Coal mining was hard and dangerous work. For Ukrainian immigrants, going into the deep, dark coal mines was a big change from the green hills and fertile fields they had known in their homeland.

Miners worked 10 or more hours per day and came home covered with black coal dust. Mines were dangerous places. Coal gave off many gases that were poisonous or explosive. Miners wore helmets with lanterns that used an open flame; often, this flame could ignite the underground gases and coal dust. The result would be an explosion, as flames swept through the mine, killing everyone in their path. Miners also had to use dynamite to blast the coal, and this could also set off a dangerous explosion.

Mines sometimes filled with water, and in many mines, miners removed as much water as coal! Water could flood mines or cause them to collapse, trapping the miners inside, where they would suffocate. Mining equipment was also dangerous. Coal cars ran through mine shafts on railroad tracks and could kill or injure miners if the cars struck them. Accidents were common and could permanently cripple victims who survived. If they survived these disasters and accidents, miners faced another killer, black lung disease, which was caused by breathing coal dust. Over time, the coal dust would ruin a miner's lungs, with fatal results.

Ukrainian and other immigrant miners were treated very poorly by the mining companies. Companies saw the miners as expendable and were not interested in improving the mines to make them safer. If a miner was killed or injured, they would simply hire another. A miner who was injured and could not work received no compensation from the company or the government. He and his family could only rely on the help of friends and relatives.

In these difficult circumstances, Ukrainian immigrants had to find creative solutions to survive and make life less difficult. One response was to form fraternal societies. These organizations were often based in Ukrainian churches. Members would contribute a certain amount of money to a central fund each month. If a member died or was injured and unable to work, the fraternal society would help the family with its expenses. Over time, these societies grew and banded together into large, national organizations that promoted Ukrainian culture, as well as providing insurance to members. The largest of these is the *Ukrainian National Association* (UNA). The UNA was founded in 1894 in Shamokin, Pennsylvania.

Miners also tried to protest the working conditions by going on strike and forming unions. Early coal miners' unions faced violence and intimidation. Coal companies did not want strikes and feared that they would lose money if they had to pay higher wages or spend more to improve safety in the mines. Coal mine owners banded together to form the Coal and Iron Police, whose job was to keep miners from protesting and to protect the companies.

In September 1897, a sheriff's posse shot and killed almost 20 striking immigrant coal miners in Lattimer, Pennsylvania. The miners were unarmed and marching peacefully behind an American flag when they were attacked. The Lattimer Massacre was one of the worst examples of labor violence in American history, but there were many smaller incidents, as well. Because of this, conditions for Ukrainian and other immigrant miners remained difficult and dangerous.

BACK TO THE LAND

Many other Ukrainian immigrants turned their backs on the hardships of life in factories and coal mines and sought a place on the land. They looked to the wide prairies of western Canada and North Dakota and saw land that resembled their native Ukraine. Governments and railroad companies owned much of the land and were eager for settlers to come and develop it. This land was often remote and not very suitable for farming. They encouraged Ukrainian settlement and tried to make the land as affordable as possible. Sometimes the railroads contacted Ukrainian priests and bishops to spread the word to potential immigrants and agreed to provide settlers with land for a church, a cemetery, and a school.

Beginning in the 1890s, thousands of Ukrainian families came to the northern Great Plains to establish farms. They often settled in isolated areas far from large cities. In many places, Ukrainians were the only settlers, so everyone spoke Ukrainian and the new arrivals could live almost as they had in the old country. What few neighbors they had were Native Americans or people of mixed Indian and French heritage called Métis.

Most farm families' first homes were dugouts with a dirt floor, covered with tree branches and roofed with sod. Their first meals were often made of wild onions, mushrooms, herbs, and a rabbit or bird they caught and roasted over an open fire. When they set about building a permanent home, they often tried to build their houses in the same patterns that they had known back in Ukraine.

The first years of settlement were the hardest for the Ukrainian farmers. Land for farming had to be cleared of brush and trees. Tough prairie sod had to be broken. Ukrainian immigrants often had to go to cities to work to earn enough to pay for the tools, seed, animals, and supplies they needed for their farms. In some cases, a husband would leave his wife and children to work the farm while he went to the city to earn extra money. One account of a Ukrainian family in Canada recalled:

> With two oxen, Magdalena plowed and cultivated a bit more land; the seeding she did by hand. That summer [her husband] Alexander sent her some money and she bought a cow. . . . Her experience of harvesting was done entirely by hand, and the help from the boys enabled her to cut, thresh, bag the wheat, stack the straw and cut some hay that was plentiful in low meadow and excellent fodder for the oxen and cow.[7]

The son of one Ukrainian immigrant to Canada remembered how his father came to his new home with little more than his strong work ethic: "He took a homestead and he was using a pick and an axe and tore it up a little at a time. That was a lot of hard work."[8]

Once trees were cut, oxen were used to pull out stumps. Rocks had to be dug up by hand. Fields were cleared bit by bit, with backbreaking work performed amid clouds of mosquitoes and biting flies.

There were other hardships to face, as well. Winter was a time of great suffering for many Ukrainian settlers. Some families barely had enough food to survive. Fierce blizzards and sub-zero temperatures kept the settlers isolated in their homes for days or weeks. In some families, the husbands went away during the winter to work in factories or logging camps. Their wives and children had to fend for themselves and became experts at surviving winter's worst.

Summer brought its own perils. Fires were the worst. During the dry months of summer, a careless campfire or a lightning strike could start a raging prairie fire. Driven by the wind, it could race across the land, destroying everything in its path: crops, homes, animals, and people. If the settlers spotted the fire coming—it would appear as a cloud of smoke above a thin red line on the horizon—they would quickly try to plow a circle around their house and barn to act as a firebreak. Families in dugout or sod houses would wrap themselves in wet blankets and hope the fire passed quickly. If the fire came suddenly, their only hope of survival was to run to the nearest creek or pond and get in the water as deep as possible.

The Ukrainian pioneers also faced diseases such as scarlet fever or diphtheria. These illnesses struck many early settlers, especially children. In many communities, a walk through the local cemetery reveals that many families lost children to the hardships of pioneer life.

Bad weather could destroy a whole year's worth of work and ruin a family. Even with good weather, the first crops of wheat were small and had to be hauled for miles to the nearest town or railroad depot before they could be sold or ground into flour. During their first years on the land, few farmers made any profit. Much of what they grew in their gardens and fields was used to feed their own families and their farm animals.

It took tremendous faith, hard work, and perseverance to merely survive the early years of settlement. Many Ukrainians had what it took. Year in and year out, Ukrainian farmers on

Ukraine is primarily made up of flat, fertile plains; consequently, many Ukrainians had been farmers prior to immigrating to the United States. Pictured here is an 18-year-old Ukrainian boy who is feeding cows on a farm, shortly after arriving in the United States in 1949.

the Great Plains overcame each challenge and made their communities a success.

BLAZING NEW TRAILS

Not all Ukrainian immigrants to North America wanted to be farmers, factory workers, or miners. Some who started out in these jobs had dreams of opening their own businesses.

In the early Ukrainian communities, one of the first businesses to open was the saloon. Saloons were places for workers to gather after work, enjoy a glass of beer, get an inexpensive meal, and meet friends. It was especially important for men who had come to America without their families and had no loved ones to go home to at night. Many saloons provided newspapers in

Ukrainian and English to their customers. Patrons could learn the news of the day, and papers were often read aloud for the benefit of those who were illiterate.

Saloonkeepers were also important figures in their communities. Opening a saloon required some political connections with local officials, and owners could use these to help their patrons. Many soon expanded their businesses to include other services that the immigrants needed: Some helped find jobs for new arrivals and others helped immigrants make travel arrangements and get steamship and train tickets for relatives who they wanted to bring over from Europe.

Ukrainian women also operated businesses in North America. The most common was the boardinghouse. While her husband worked at his job in a factory or mine, the wife would cook, clean, and keep house for workers who did not yet have families in America. This brought in extra income that helped the family make it through tough times, but the work was very demanding. One Ukrainian writer described how hard a boarding housekeeper worked every day:

> From early in the morning to late in the evening, she is always on her feet, always working in miserable, perpetual, and monotonous boredom. She awakens in the morning and prepares breakfast for her boarders; then she washes the dishes and cleans the house; later she cooks supper and again she washes the dishes and cleans the house; in her spare moments she washes the boarders' clothes. . . . And so it goes, day after day. All that and children too![9]

In cities with large garment factories, such as New York City, Ukrainian women also worked as seamstresses. Sometimes, they worked in sweatshop factories, but whenever possible they used their sewing skills to supplement their family's income. Some simply began to work from home and later expanded into small businesses.

Ukrainian immigrants soon discovered that their favorite foods weren't available in the stores in North America. In cities, as Ukrainian communities grew, many working families did not have the time or money to prepare delicacies such as Ukrainian sausage. Some enterprising immigrants began to open Ukrainian restaurants, delis, bakeries, and even small companies to produce the foods that their fellow immigrants wanted.

Because Ukrainians had often been denied education and knowledge of their history and culture in Europe, printing and publishing was also an important activity in larger Ukrainian communities. Ukrainian publishers produced books, magazines, and newspapers. These covered every topic imaginable. They reprinted the works of Ukrainian authors such as Shevchenko and Franko, as well as translations of American and British writers. There were also practical works, such as "how-to" guides, and histories of Ukraine, the United States, and Canada.

A NEW WAVE

Immigrants who have come from Ukraine in the past 25 years have not followed in the footsteps of earlier Ukrainian immigrants. Few of these recent immigrants became farmers or coal miners. They arrived in North America with more education than the first wave of Ukrainians, and, as a result, they tried to look for jobs that fit their educational background. Like the earlier immigrants, however, not being able to speak English limited the jobs that some could take. Some new arrivals became construction workers, maids, janitors, and taxicab drivers.

Still, they sought to better themselves. Once they learned English, they began to move more quickly into their old professions or they went to school to learn new professions. They became nurses, doctors, dentists, salespeople, real estate agents, travel agents, and designers, just to name a few of the professions in which recent immigrants have excelled. Others began to open small businesses. Since Ukraine gained independence, some have used their contacts with Ukraine to open businesses that import Ukrainian goods.

In recent years, one small but important group of immigrants has been students and professors. Since Ukraine gained independence, college students and teachers have been able to come to the United States or Canada to attend school. Professors have come to teach or as part of an exchange program in which North American professors trade places with a Ukrainian colleague for a year. These temporary immigrants gain new knowledge and learn new skills that they can take back to Ukraine in order to help their country build a brighter future.

Regardless of where they settled, whether on farms in western Canada, in the coal-mining regions of Pennsylvania, or in industrial cities like New York, Chicago, Cleveland, or Detroit, Ukrainian immigrants came to North America and rolled up their sleeves and went to work. Jobs and businesses provided a living that made it possible to escape the poverty they had known in the old country and a way to bring their families to America and build a better life for their children.

Still, finding a job and getting settled was just the beginning of their new lives. To preserve their heritage and faith, they also needed strong communities that would ensure that their values would live on for generations to come.

• Study Questions •

1. List some of the major locations in North America where Ukrainian immigrants settled.

2. What was life like for a Ukrainian coal miner in Pennsylvania?

3. What were some of the hardships that Ukrainian pioneers faced in western Canada?

4. What jobs did more recent Ukrainian immigrants take compared to the earlier generation?

5

Making a
New Home

Ukrainian life in North America has always revolved around the home and the community. After they immigrated, the new arrivals had to find a place to settle and look for jobs. At the same time, they looked for ways to make their new lives easier. They faced the loneliness of being far from family and friends, and language barriers had to be overcome. Life on the farm and in the coal mines and factories was hard. Although more recent arrivals from Ukraine had it a little easier, they, too, faced a difficult adjustment.

Ukrainians came to North America for a better life. They wanted to keep their culture, faith, and traditions while enjoying the freedom their adopted homelands offered. To do all these things and to make their new surroundings seem more like home, Ukrainian immigrants needed to form communities.

FINDING HOME

The building block of the Ukrainian community was the family. In the family home, the culture and traditions of immigrant life were transmitted to a new generation. Those who came to America as children and those children who were born to Ukrainian immigrant parents had no personal memories of life in Ukraine. Their ideas of what it meant to be Ukrainian were created in North America.

In the old country, families could rely on a network of grandparents, aunts and uncles, cousins, and neighbors to help teach their children cultural traditions. In North America, families were on their own. In many cases, immigrants to North America were young people who had not had the opportunity to fully absorb the traditions of their parents and grandparents.

Keeping Ukrainian traditions alive was a struggle, especially during important holidays such as Easter and Christmas. How did mother and grandmother make the delicious Easter bread called *pashka*? What were the words to the songs father used to sing at Christmastime? How can we find the ingredients to make the foods we remember from childhood? What were the recipes? All of these questions had to be answered.

In many families, keeping Ukrainian culture alive was the job of wives and mothers. Husbands and fathers were often working long hours on the farm or in factories or mines. At home, women worked just as hard as men did outside the home (if not harder). Because so many traditions occurred in and around the family home, it fell to these women to teach their children Ukrainian customs.

Some traditions had to be adjusted to fit the new American realities. Others could be preserved "just as in the old country." Parents did not have their own parents to turn to for advice, so they had to depend on friends and neighbors and they had to work more closely with their children. Children had new roles and responsibilities in helping the family maintain its traditions.

One example was the date for Christmas. In the Eastern Christian tradition, Christmas is celebrated on January 7 rather than on December 25, as in the Western Christian tradition. Early immigrants to North America faced a difficult choice. Public schools and many employers refused to allow January 7 as a day off for Ukrainians. Some Ukrainians switched the date of their celebration of Christmas to December, but others kept it in January.

In some cases, Ukrainian immigrants discovered modern conveniences that made it easier for them to preserve their culture. According to one author, on farms in Canada "the Ukrainian women no longer gather plants, barks, and mosses to make their dyes [for clothing]. They find they can produce the colours they want by using commercial dyes—and who can blame them for so lightening their labours?"[10]

Other traditions could be preserved from Ukraine. The custom of decorating Easter eggs—called *pysanky*—was one example. One woman, the daughter of Ukrainian immigrants from Canada, recalled:

> Mother taught us girls how to decorate Easter eggs. She didn't make them too fancy, just simple. As long as there was a line around and some leaf. You see, they believed very much in all that from the old country. The line that encircles the egg has no beginning and no end so it symbolizes eternity. And a pine tree, she always made a pine tree to signify eternal youth and health. She made roosters, eternity and fulfillment of wishes and always a fish for Christianity. Mother never made reindeers, but other people did. They must have come from a different village. The dyes were all from the old country, beautiful dyes.[11]

In more recent years, popular customs associated with the Ukrainian Christmas Eve were streamlined: The traditional importance of barn animals was dropped, and hay strewn under

Like Christmas, Easter is one of the primary holidays celebrated by Ukrainians. Decorated Easter eggs—known as pysanky—are among the most important traditions of this holiday and are colorfully decorated using the wax-resistant method known as batik.

the table disappeared. Because most Ukrainians in North America no longer live in separate Ukrainian colonies, impromptu house-to-house caroling has become less common and is now sometimes used as a fund-raiser for churches or organizations.

Easter

The most important religious holiday in Ukraine has always been Easter. Easter commemorates and honors the death and resurrection of Jesus Christ. Because it occurs during the spring, Easter is also a time to look forward to the rebirth of nature after the winter. It is preceded by Lent, a 40-day period of fasting, repentance, and reflection. During this time, Ukrainians did not eat meat on Fridays and did not have parties, dances, or weddings. They tried to make amends to friends, family, or neighbors with whom they had had arguments or hard feelings.

Palm Sunday (Shutkova Nedilia) began the Holy Week of Easter. To commemorate Christ's entry into Jerusalem, Ukrainian immigrants would carry pussy willow branches to church to be blessed. (These were used because palm fronds were rare and hard to get in Ukraine and the early immigrant communities in North America.) Sometimes, Ukrainian immigrants would tap each other with the branches and recite poems that reminded themselves that Easter would soon arrive.

For Ukrainian immigrants in North America, the week before Easter was a time of intense preparation. There was special food to be made, and the house had to be completely cleaned. Extra care went into making Easter bread, or pashka. Cooks had to think only positive thoughts while baking this bread, and strangers were not allowed into the house during the cooking because they might hex the pashka. It was said that only pashkas made in this way could turn out light, airy, and delicious.

This was the time when Ukrainian families colored beautiful pysanky. The symbols inscribed on the eggs reflected the themes of Easter—eternal life, rebirth, and the renewal of nature. The most popular method of decorating pysanky is the use of the wax-resistant method, or *batik*. A specialized instrument called the *kistka*, or *ryl'tse*, is used to draw the design with hot wax. The dyes used in the process also had a symbolic meaning. Red symbolized the sun, life, and joy; yellow stood for wealth and fertility; and green was the symbol of spring and plant life. In the past, artists prepared their own dyes using the bark of oak or ash trees, twigs of sour apple trees, saffron, or willow tree leaves. In more recent times, chemical dyes have been used.

Good Friday was the most solemn day of Holy Week. Like Christians around the world, Ukrainian immigrants fasted and went to church to remember Christ's death. Ukrainian Catholic and Orthodox churches would have a *plashchenytsia*, a model of Christ's tomb, set up in the church, where the faithful would go to pray. The next day, Holy Saturday, there were more preparations for Easter. Ukrainian families would fill a special basket full of Easter foods—eggs, sweet bread (pashka), kovbasa, cheese, and spicy horseradish. They would go to church, which would fill with fellow immigrants, and the priest would bless the food. Many children recall how the church would fill up with the delicious smells of Easter as the priest sprinkled each basket with holy water—but the food couldn't be eaten yet!

Early on Easter morning, families would rise, put on their best clothes, and go to church to celebrate the Mass of the Resurrection. Afterward, they would greet friends and neighbors with hugs and three kisses each and then would hurry home to the Easter breakfast that consisted of all the dishes prepared during Holy Week. The centerpiece of each table would be the Easter pashka, which was covered with symbols made of dough such as a cross, solar signs, rosettes, leaves, pine cones, birds, or bees. After the meal, time was spent singing, dancing, and enjoying being with one's family and friends.

Christmas

Although Easter was the most important holiday, Christmas was often the favorite holiday of Ukrainians in Ukraine and in North America. The Christmas season began with the Feast of St. Nicholas (December 6 or December 19, depending on which calendar they used), when someone dressed up as the famous saint, sometimes accompanied by helper "angels" who would visit families and quiz the children on their knowledge of religion. Children would receive small gifts, perhaps pieces of fruit or candy. In Ukraine and in early Ukrainian immigrant communities in North America, the main day for gift giving was St. Nicholas Day rather than Christmas Day itself.

In more recent times, as Ukrainian communities have become more modernized, this custom has been replaced with St. Nicholas parties. Instead of having the saint visit each child's home, the children of the Ukrainian community gather at their local churches and Ukrainian halls and meet St. Nicholas there. In most families, gift giving is now most common on Christmas Day.

Ukrainian Christmas celebrations begin on Christmas Eve (December 24 or January 6, depending on the calendar) and continue through the Feast of the Three Kings, 12 days later. On Christmas Eve, there is intense preparation and excitement as a special evening meal is prepared. On farms, children gather a little hay from the manger to place under the tablecloth at the dinner table. (Even families that live in the city usually manage to find a little hay or straw for this custom.) The younger children are usually distracted from excitement by being given the important task of going outside to watch for the first star.

When the first star is visible in the night sky, Christmas Eve begins and the family gathers around the table. In addition to place settings for the family, it is customary to set out an extra place to remember family members who have passed away or for any guest who might arrive unannounced. The head of the family—traditionally the father—breaks a piece of bread and gives a piece dipped in honey to each member of the family. The bread is eaten, and everyone wishes each other a merry Christmas.

The Christmas Eve meal consists of 12 dishes, all of which are meatless. In the middle of the table is an elaborately braided sweet bread called *kolach*, with a candle placed in the center.

Other symbolic foods include *kutia* (wheat porridge mixed with poppy seeds and honey) and *uzvar*, a drink made from stewed fruit. After these, more dishes are served: *borscht* (beet soup) with *vushka* (dumplings filled with chopped mushrooms), followed by a variety of fish—baked, broiled, fried, cold in aspic (a clear jelly), fish balls, and pickled herring—then varenyky (pierogi filled with cabbage, potatoes, or prunes) and *holubtsi* (stuffed cabbage).

After dinner, it is time for Christmas carols. In early immigrant communities, it was common for people to go door to door singing traditional Ukrainian Christmas songs just as they had in the old country. Then, the family changed for church and, bundled against the cold, would go to midnight Mass. Afterward, a second meal was eaten, small gifts were distributed, and more Christmas songs were sung, sometimes until the next morning! This joyful time of song and good food would continue for 12 days. This tradition was carried on mostly in rural communities, where the winter season provided a little more free time. Many of the immigrants who worked in factories or mines had to go back to work, although they kept the spirit of the season alive by singing and enjoying themselves when they came home after a day of hard work.

CHURCHES

Like many immigrants, early Ukrainian immigrants were deeply religious, and most significant customs and traditions involved religion. Strong faith helped Ukrainian peasants overcome their hardships with patience and good cheer and helped them make sense of a world that often seemed hostile toward them. Churches provided a sense of identity and purpose. They helped preserve Ukrainian traditions, culture, and language in North America.

For early Ukrainian immigrants, building a church was the first big community effort in which they became involved. It would provide a place of worship, a place to socialize and meet neighbors, a location to gather, and, later, a place to establish other community groups. The first churches built by the new arrivals were often very simple wooden chapels. One Ukrainian Canadian remembered:

> Our church was just a small wooden one. There were no pews. You stood for the two and a half hours of the mass.

HOW TO MAKE UKRAINIAN-STYLE BORSCHT

Soup holds a special place in Ukrainian cuisine, and it often seems as if no proper meal can be complete with at least a cup of soup. In the summer, soups can be chilled and refreshing. In the winter, they are warm and filling.

Borscht is one of the favorite soups of Ukraine. It is eaten in many countries of eastern and central Europe. Borscht (or barshch) is named after its main ingredient, beets.

There are endless varieties of borscht, ranging from a simple broth to a hearty stewlike dish that can be served with fresh bread as a meal. Ukrainian borscht is usually a hearty soup filled with meat and vegetables. It goes best with a good crusty rye or pumpernickel bread.

This recipe calls for about a pound of beets. You can use canned beets with their juice or fresh beets. If you use fresh beets, try roasting them in a 300-degree oven until they are slightly caramelized and then peel and dice them. Roasting brings out the natural sweetness of the beets.

BORSCHT
Ingredients
1 carrot, diced
1 celery stalk, sliced
1/4 small head of cabbage, shredded
2 potatoes, diced
6 cups beef, chicken, or vegetable broth
1 lb. beets

No choir, just a *dyak* [cantor] and some singers. There were religious pictures with paper flowers around them. A group of girls would get together before Easter and scrub the floors and make these flowers. It was so cold in there during the winter! There was just a wood burning heater that they would start up on Saturday but even so your feet froze during the service.[12]

1/2 cup plain baked beans, rinsed
4 tomatoes, chopped
1 tbsp. instant flour
2 tbsp. cold water
Garlic powder
1 tbsp. lemon juice
1/2 tsp. sugar
1/8 tsp. pepper
Salt
1/2 cup sour cream (optional)

Simmer carrots, celery, cabbage, and potatoes in the broth for 20 minutes. Add beets (with juice if using canned beets), beans, and tomatoes. Cook for five minutes. Add the flour mixed with the cold water. Cook for five minutes.

Remove from heat and season with garlic powder, lemon juice, sugar, pepper, and salt. If desired, add a spoonful of sour cream in the bowl just before serving.

Hint: Borscht often tastes even better a day after it is made, so it can be made and then stored overnight in the refrigerator and reheated. If you make it ahead of time, leave out the sour cream until just before serving.

From these humble origins, Ukrainian communities gradually enlarged and expanded their churches. In urban communities, where there were more people to support a large parish church, impressive structures of brick began to rise in Ukrainian neighborhoods, decorated inside with glorious icons and stained-glass windows. Despite coming from intense poverty, Ukrainian immigrants built their churches to last, hiring the best architects and builders. They often sought out renowned icon painters to make holy pictures for their sanctuary. By building such beautiful churches, they were telling everyone who passed by that they were putting down roots in North America and were putting their stamp on the community.

Because the church was the first and usually most important place in the Ukrainian community, the priest was often among the most respected leaders. His advice on spiritual, family, and legal matters was often sought. In poor communities, the priest lived alongside the people, sharing their daily toils. One immigrant from Canada remembered:

> The priests in those days had a hard time. They worked hard for us and were poor, God bless them. The roads were bad, the parishes didn't have much money, they had to get around in a wagon even in bad weather. Our priest would play the violin for us at christenings, drop in for a visit and a drink of whiskey, help out with the shocking or shoveling grain. What can I say? A good man.[13]

DIVIDED TRADITIONS

The early waves of Ukrainian immigrants did not always view themselves as Ukrainians. Their main loyalties were to their families, churches, and home villages. Ukraine did not exist as a nation, and there were few opportunities to learn about Ukrainian history or literature. Aside from the language, stories, and traditions they learned at home, when they arrived in North America few Ukrainians were aware of what it meant to be Ukrainian.

The church is an integral part of Ukrainian communities
in the United States, and priests are the most important
figures in the Ukrainian Catholic Church. Pictured here is
Stefan Soroka, who was installed as the sixth metropolitan-
archbishop of the Ukrainian Catholic Archeparchy of
Philadelphia—the highest position in the United States—
in 2001.

For the first time in their adopted homelands, the immigrants had the freedom to learn about where they came from. As their status slowly improved, they had a little extra money to spend on Ukrainian cultural items, especially books, newspapers, and music. Many communities opened their own schools to teach their American-born children their ancestral language, history, and culture.

The journey to North America forced immigrants to answer new questions. In North America, they encountered many other ethnic and racial groups from throughout the world. Ukrainians had to ask themselves, "What does it mean to be Ukrainian?" Not all immigrants from Ukraine came up with the same answer. How they responded had a lot to do with where they came from in Ukraine and what church they belonged to.

Carpatho-Rusyns

Among the first immigrants from Ukraine in North America were Carpatho-Rusyns (also called Ruthenians). They came from the Carpathian Mountains of far western Ukraine, where they lived as shepherds and farmers. They came from three groups: Lemkos, Hutsuls, and Bojkos. Each group spoke a slightly different dialect, although they could all understand each other. Because they lived in the mountains and far from any major city, Carpatho-Rusyns were separated from the surrounding Ukrainian, Polish, and Slovak cultures. They consider themselves a unique and separate group.

Most Carpatho-Rusyns belong to the Eastern-rite Catholic Church. This church is part of the Roman Catholic Church but uses Orthodox-style religious services and its priests are permitted to marry. (It is also known as the Greek or Byzantine Catholic Church.) When the Carpatho-Rusyns first arrived in North America, there were few Eastern-rite Catholic churches to which they could belong. Some joined Slovak, Hungarian, or Polish Roman Catholic churches. Others formed their own churches.

The Ruthenian Catholics, who largely come from the Carpathian Mountain region of western Ukraine, are part of the Eastern-rite Catholic Church and thus are not part of the Ukrainian Catholic Church. Pictured here are Pope John Paul II and Judson M. Procyk, who served as metropolitan of the Byzantine Catholic Archdiocese of Pittsburgh from 1995 to 2001.

Many of the early immigrants came from a part of the Carpathian Mountains ruled by the Kingdom of Hungary. These immigrants called themselves Uhro-Rusyn, which means "Hungarian-Rusyn," and formed their own Catholic churches. Immigrants from the north side of the mountains, ruled by Austria, called themselves either Carpatho-Rusyn or Ukrainian. Those who came from the highland regions were the most likely to call themselves "Rusyns." Those from the lowlands and valleys were more likely to call themselves "Ukrainian."

The early immigrants to North America could not agree on what to call themselves. They separated according to where they came from, what church they belonged to, and what type of government they thought should eventually rule their homeland. This confusion was made more acute by the actions of some American Catholic bishops, many of whom were Irish Americans. Often, these bishops did not want to provide separate churches for these newcomers. They also felt that it would be better if the immigrants spoke English and stopped practicing customs from the old country. The bishops wanted the Catholic Church to be accepted by other Americans and were afraid of seeming too "foreign" or "different."

Russian Orthodoxy

In 1890, a more serious conflict arose in Minnesota. A small community of Eastern Catholic Ukrainian/Rusyn immigrants had built a church in Minneapolis. Their first pastor was Father Alexis Toth. On arriving in Minneapolis, Father Toth went to introduce himself to the local Catholic bishop. Bishop John Ireland was one of the most influential bishops in the United States and was against immigrants who wanted to keep their own language and culture. He treated Father Toth very rudely. The two priests began to argue; the archbishop ordered Father Toth to leave and refused to grant permission for his new church to operate.

Disgusted with his treatment, Father Toth soon made contact with the Russian Orthodox bishop of San Francisco. At that time, there was no separate Ukrainian Orthodox Church in the United States. He and his parish then converted to the Russian Orthodox faith. Soon, Father Toth convinced Rusyns in other

cities to leave the Catholic Church and join the Russian Orthodox Church.

Those who followed Father Toth's movement began to
worship in Russian. They spoke Russian and began to identify
with Russian culture. In time, most stopped calling themselves
Ukrainian or Rusyn and simply referred to themselves as Russian, even though their ancestors had never lived in Russia!

Ukrainian Orthodox Church

The Ukrainian Autocephalous Orthodox Church in North
America was founded during the second wave of immigration
from Ukraine in the 1920s. The Ukrainians who joined this
church were both new immigrants and children of the earlier
wave of immigrants. This Orthodox Church had to overcome
many obstacles to gain acceptance from other churches, including fellow Orthodox Churches in Europe. Alternative Ukrainian Orthodox Churches were founded in the United States and
Canada.

These churches had a hard time cooperating with one another. Each had its own leaders, and their goals and personalities often clashed. The most influential Orthodox Church,
based in Constantinople, Turkey, also failed to assist by recog-
nizing these churches. Because of this, the Ukrainian Orthodox
faith in America remained weak and divided.

Ukrainian Protestants

Most Ukrainians were either Orthodox or Catholic. Small
groups of Ukrainian Protestants also made their home in North
America, however. Among the first to immigrate were a group
of *Stundists* (also called Pavlovtsy), who were pacifists from
north-central Ukraine. They came to North America to escape
persecution. Because they opposed all forms of violence, they
would not join the army. This angered the leaders of the Russian
Orthodox Church and the government who saw the Stundists

as disloyal to Russia. In 1899, many began to immigrate to the United States and Canada, settling as farmers in North Dakota, Saskatchewan, and other areas. Groups of Baptists and Presbyterians from Ukraine also made their way to the United States during these years.

For Ukrainian immigrants, the family and the church were the building blocks of community life. Ukraine's turbulent history was echoed in the divide among the many different churches that strove to serve the community. Although they did not bring all Ukrainians together, they did help the immigrants find a common community in North America.

• Study Questions •

1. How did Ukrainian immigrants keep some of their traditions alive?
   ....

2. How did some of their customs change in North America?
   ....

3. Why were churches a vital part of Ukrainian immigrant life?
   ....

4. Who are Carpatho-Rusyns?
   ....

6

Bringing Ukrainian Traditions to North America

Ukrainians in the United States and Canada created many community organizations. These groups were founded because immigrants wanted to preserve their culture and also because they needed services that other organizations could not or would not provide.

DISCRIMINATION

Ukrainian immigrants in both Canada and the United States suffered from discrimination. As new immigrants, they could not speak English and were often forced to take the toughest, dirtiest jobs—such as working in coal mines. Native-born Americans and Canadians sometimes saw Ukrainians as too "different" or strange. Many believed that Ukrainians were so different that they would never be good citizens, and many also opposed allowing Ukrainians to teach public school or gain positions of public trust. In many instances, Ukrainians were called "Russians" and described as lesser than people of white English stock.

One newspaper in Canada printed the following, which objected to the appointment of Ukrainians as local district officials:

> It is quite possible that English-speaking generations yet unborn will come to look upon the descendants of Galician [Ukrainian] immigrants as their equals and friends; at the present time we do not so consider them. In view of their education, ideas, moral standards, and way of life, we justly regard them as inferiors. We are prepared to treat them with fairness and civility; we are not prepared to be bossed by them. . . . When it comes to investing a Russian yokel with authority to dictate, in the Government's name, to English-speaking British subjects, we think this is going too far. . . . We resent it as a humiliation; and it is unlikely that white men in this Province will stand for it.[14]

Although nonwhite immigrant groups such as the Chinese usually suffered even worse discrimination, feelings against immigrants from eastern and southern Europe were very strong. At the same time, there were also many in the United States and Canada who welcomed Ukrainians as willing workers and new neighbors.

The Internment, 1914–1920

Prejudice against Ukrainians sometimes led to serious injustice. The worst example was the imprisonment of Ukrainians in Canada during World War I. When the war broke out in 1914, Canada joined Great Britain on the side of the Allied powers. Ukrainians who came from Galicia had been subjects of Austria-Hungary, which was one of Canada's and Great Britain's enemies. Few Ukrainians were loyal to Austria-Hungary and had come to North America to be free of Austrian or Russian rule, but this did not matter to the Canadian government. Prejudice against Ukrainians and wartime tensions led many Canadians to view their new Ukrainian neighbors with fear and mistrust.

In 1914, the Canadian government passed a decree that allowed authorities to imprison citizens of Austria-Hungary as enemies in 26 special camps located throughout the country. More than 5,000 Ukrainians, including some who were Canadian citizens, were imprisoned by this order. Most of those detained were men, but there were also women and children in the camps. The Ukrainian prisoners often had their homes and other property taken away for no reason. Approximately 80,000 more Ukrainians were subject to special government restrictions and had to register with local police wherever they went.

While in the camps, the Ukrainians caught up in these internment operations were transported to Canada's remotest areas, where they were forced to work on heavy labor projects such as road building, clearing land, and drainage projects, often under very difficult conditions. One of the areas where they worked was the famous Banff National Park. Prisoners were denied access to newspapers, and their correspondence was censored and limited. They were forced not only to maintain the camps but to work for the government and private concerns, and they were sometimes mistreated by the guards. About 69 Ukrainians died of mistreatment and poor conditions while in the camps.

There was never any evidence of disloyalty on the part of Ukrainian Canadians. Many served in the Canadian armed forces, often with great courage. One such example was Sergeant Philip Konowal. He joined the 47th Canadian Infantry Battalion of the Canadian Expeditionary Force and fought with exceptional valor in combat in August 1917. For his actions, Konowal was awarded the Victoria Cross—the highest decoration of the British Empire—by King George V in London on October 15, 1917. Ironically, at the same time that Canada was being honored by Konowal's achievements, it was treating other Ukrainians with great injustice.

MAKING A COMMUNITY

Faced with many challenges in North America, Ukrainian immigrants responded with creativity and hard work. The result was the formation of many organizations that together made up strong Ukrainian communities. Many of these organizations have survived successfully for decades and have been joined by new organizations.

The first institution in most communities was the church (discussed in Chapter 5). Once a church had been built, other groups soon followed. The first to be founded were usually parish church societies. There were groups for men, women, and young people. Many of the early church societies were founded to assist the parish or for prayer and religious observances. They also provided a place to meet and socialize.

During holidays and festivals, these societies would often march in processions around the church or in the immediate area. These processions were very colorful and popular activities. Members of each society would dress in their best clothes and usually had a pin or sash to identify their group. Each group had a banner, usually with a picture of a saint embroidered on it. With the priest, cantors, and choir, the societies would march in honor of the holiday.

Church societies also took on another important task—helping members who were facing some personal or family crisis, such as an injury, death in the family, or loss of a job. As these societies took on more and more of these problems, Ukrainian immigrants started to realize the need for some form of *fraternal insurance* to help members in time of need. From this idea, the Ukrainian fraternal movement in North America was born.

Fraternal Societies

Fraternal insurance was created by people who could not afford standard life insurance. Immigrants and others who worked in dangerous industries such as coal mining were considered too great a risk for insurance, so most companies would not sell them policies. Because of this, Ukrainian immigrants who were injured or killed on the job left their families in poverty. In the early days of industry, there were no pensions, sick days, or worker's compensation. If you could not work, you did not get paid. Like many immigrant groups, Ukrainians began to band together to create their own low-cost insurance societies.

The first fraternal societies grew from churches. Members would pay a small fee every month, and the money was placed in a special account. If a member died or was injured, this money was used to help the member's family pay bills, buy food, or even pay for a proper funeral. Societies also made sure that all of their members were good citizens, behaved themselves, and supported the Ukrainian community in its activities. As an early Ukrainian activist said, "One person cannot help everyone, but everyone can help one person."

Soon, these small societies started to band together to form larger federations. These larger fraternal federations allowed a member who moved from one community to another to retain his insurance. Because more people could join, the larger fraternal societies were more stable and could provide more benefits. Fraternal societies became nationwide Ukrainian organizations and were able to represent the needs and wishes of many Ukrainians in politics or the media.

The first and largest Ukrainian fraternal society was the aforementioned Ukrainian National Association, or UNA. During its first year—1894—the organization had just 439 members. Ten years later, that number had grown to 5,878. By 1974, UNA had more than 89,000 members, making it the largest Ukrainian organization in the free world. The UNA began in the United States, but in 1901 it also began to accept Canadian citizens as members. In addition to caring for its members, the goals of the UNA are to unite all Ukrainians in the United States and Canada, and to promote the culture and well-being of the Ukrainian community in North America.

Like many fraternal societies, the UNA is divided into local branches in each area where there are Ukrainians. All the branches in a particular area are grouped into districts. The national headquarters is in Newark, New Jersey.

Other organizations soon followed the UNA, many of them oriented toward young people or women. The Ukrainian National Women's League of America (UNWLA) was founded in 1925. The UNWLA later founded the Ukrainian Museum in New York as a center for Ukrainian culture. In the 1930s, the Ukrainian Youth League of North America was established to promote Ukrainian culture and heritage among the children of the original immigrants.

The Ukrainian Museum in New York City was founded by the Ukrainian National Women's League of America (UNWLA) in 1976 and is home to an extensive collection of Ukrainian costumes, ceramics, art, and photographs. The museum was designed to preserve Ukraine's rich cultural heritage through interpretive and educational programs.

Education

Schools and learning have always been important to Ukrainian immigrants. North America provided them with an opportunity to teach their culture and faith to their children, an opportunity that most did not have before. The first education efforts began in the 1890s, when many Ukrainian churches set up reading rooms for immigrants. These were small libraries with books and newspapers that people could come to read for free or for a small fee.

Later, many churches organized grade schools for children. These offered classes in both Ukrainian and English. Students learned both American and Ukrainian history and literature along with subjects such as math, religion, and music. Ukrainians also founded night schools and Saturday schools for workers and others who could not attend schools during the day but still wanted to learn. In the 1930s and 1940s, Ukrainians successfully convinced some American universities to offer Ukrainian language courses and, later, classes on history and literature for college students. In the 1960s, Ukrainian organizations helped to start a program of Ukrainian studies at Harvard University.

Newspapers and Books

Ukrainian immigrants in Canada and the United States founded many newspapers. As mentioned previously, the first newspaper published by a Ukrainian immigrant was founded by Reverend Agapius Honcharenko in 1868. It was titled the *Alaska Herald* and, in addition to being one of Alaska's first newspapers, was also the first North American newspaper to publish articles about Ukrainian history and literature. The first newspaper entirely in Ukrainian was *Amerika*, founded in 1886 by Father Ivan Wolansky. The largest and most influential paper was called *Svoboda* ("Freedom"). It has been published in Ukrainian by the UNA since 1894. Since 1933, the UNA has also published the *Ukrainian Weekly* in English.

Many Ukrainian organizations sponsored their own newspapers. Some were meant to support a political viewpoint such as Communism, Socialism, or Nationalism; others were published by a particular church for its members.

There were also children's and youth newspapers and magazines in both Ukrainian and English. Some had text in both languages so young people could practice their language skills. The best-known Ukrainian-American children's magazine is *Veselka* ("Rainbow"), which was first published in 1954. It contains poetry, stories, legends, factual articles, memoirs, puzzles, and jokes.

To promote Ukrainian education, many organizations and newspapers also started to publish books about Ukrainian topics for immigrants and their children, as well as for non-Ukrainians in Canada and the United States. Some were how-to pamphlets, such as instructions to help immigrants get their citizenship papers or learn basic English. Many organizations promoted citizenship and printed histories of the United States and Canada, as well as copies of the U.S. Constitution and Declaration of Independence in Ukrainian. In the 1940s, many Ukrainian organizations started to publish books of Ukrainian history and literature that would not have been available in North America otherwise. In 1963, the UNA sponsored the publication of a two-volume encyclopedia of Ukraine.

Dance, Theater, and Music Groups

The first Ukrainian folk dance troupes were founded around the time of World War II. Since then, Ukrainian dance has continued to grow in popularity. Canada alone is home to dozens of Ukrainian dance groups. Groups perform vibrant, acrobatic dances such as the *hopak*—called the most exciting folk dance in the world—to graceful, stylized, romantic movements in *kokhanochka*. The first Ukrainian dance groups performed for local audiences. Since the 1970s, however, many have adopted professional choreography and tour North America every summer.

Theater was another way for Ukrainians in North America to express their culture. Early theater groups were based in local Ukrainian churches. Members often wrote their own plays, designed costumes and sets, and promoted the plays themselves. They dealt with themes from immigrant life and Ukrainian history and legend.

Music has always played a special role in Ukrainian life in North America. From the first immigrants to the present, Ukrainians expressed their culture in songs and instrumental performances. Church choirs were the first organized musical groups, but they were soon followed by bands, ensembles, and folk choirs. In addition to these expressions of Ukrainian culture, there have also been Ukrainian recording studios, radio programs, and, more recently, television programs.

Festivals

In the years after World War II, Ukrainians became more a part of the mainstream culture of Canada and the United States. Many stopped living in Ukrainian neighborhoods. Because of this, daily contact with fellow Ukrainians was not as common. Parents worried that their children would not learn or appreciate their cultural roots.

To fill this gap, many Ukrainian communities in North America started yearly cultural festivals. Some of these began in the years after the war, but as new immigrants have come from Ukraine, new festivals have sprung up across the United States and Canada. Festivals often feature music, folk dance, Ukrainian food, contests, and pageants.

Many of the festivals are very successful. The Montreal Ukrainian Festival, held every September since 1999, is the largest Ukrainian event of its kind in Quebec and attracts more than 12,000 people. The festival showcases Ukrainian culture to the general population, and it is also an opportunity to learn more about Ukrainian heritage. Another example is Michigan's Ukrainian Sunflower Festival, which started in 1986. It is among

(continues on page 92)

UKRAINIAN MUSIC IN NORTH AMERICA

There is an old Ukrainian saying: "Bring together two Ukrainians, and you have the beginnings of another choir."

Music has played a significant role in Ukrainian culture. Because instrumental music is not used in Orthodox Church services, a chorus of singers provides music for the liturgy. Choral music in the Eastern Christian world became a powerful form of cultural and religious expression. Ukrainian choruses are especially well known around the world for their skill and tonal richness. Most Ukrainian communities have at least one church choir, and many have several choirs and choruses that perform popular and folk music.

In traditional Ukrainian music, the same melody is distributed among different voice parts, with one leading voice. The lead singer (*zaspivoovach*) determines the melody and the other voices come in later. This form of singing is often embellished by an independent voice in a very high register (*vyvodtshyk*). Ukrainian singing allows the principal voice much space for creativity and variation in both words and music.

One of the best-known Ukrainian choruses is Vesnivka, founded in Toronto in 1965. This choir has performed throughout North America and in Europe. It has won many awards in Canada and Europe.

Ukrainian music has helped influence the history of American music as well. The Christmas carol "Carol of the Bells," performed by many choruses during the holidays, is of Ukrainian origin. Dinah Shore's 1940 hit "Yes, My Darling Daughter," which sold more than one million copies, is based on a Ukrainian folk tune. Ukrainian musicians were among the first to popularize recordings of polka music. One of the most famous Ukrainian-American musicians was Pawlo Humeniuk. He was born in Ukraine and immigrated to the United States as a boy. Humeniuk was a self-taught fiddler who helped create modern polka music as a popular dance form. He was among the first recording stars of polka. In the 1920s, some of his albums may have sold as many as 100,000 copies!

Outside of the church, another form of Ukrainian music was provided by bandurists. The bandura is a stringed instrument with an ancient history. Early forms of the bandura existed as far back as the sixth century. Modern banduras come in several forms with 20 to 65 strings. The classical bandura is tuned diatonically and has 20 strings and wooden pegs; the Kharkiv bandura is tuned diatonically or chromatically and has a single string mechanism and 34 to 65 strings; and the Kyiv bandura, which has 55 to 64 strings, is tuned chromatically. The bandura has long been known as the national instrument of Ukraine. Early bandurists were often blind and traveled around the country singing heroic epics of Ukrainian history and folklore. During the Soviet period, many bandurists were executed or imprisoned for helping to keep Ukrainian culture alive.

When Ukrainian immigrants came to North America, they brought these musical traditions. During the Soviet era, Ukrainians were more able to perform and teach their music in North America than in their homeland. Traditions that were banned by the Soviet government in Ukraine were preserved by Ukrainian immigrants.

In 1949, a group of Ukrainian Americans and Canadians and recent refugees from Ukraine formed the Ukrainian Bandurist Chorus in Detroit. (It was originally founded in Ukraine in 1918, but Soviet authorities disbanded the chorus.) Many of the early members worked in auto factories during the day and practiced and performed their music in evenings and on weekends. The chorus performed for noted personalities such as former presidents Richard Nixon and Ronald Reagan, movie star Jack Palance, and the former president of Ukraine, Leonid Kravchuk.

Today, as new generations of Ukrainian immigrants arrive in North America to join the descendants of earlier waves of immigration, music provides a common bond that brings together the newcomers and the established Ukrainian Americans and Canadians.

The Pysanka festival in Vegreville, Alberta, has been held each July since 1973 and celebrates Ukrainian culture through music, dance, and food. Pictured here are Ukrainian dancers performing in front of the world's largest pysanka, or Easter egg, at the festival.

(continued from page 89)

the most popular and largest ethnic summer festivals in Michigan, attracting 25,000 people every year. The festival features Ukrainian food, ethnic dancing in traditional costumes, and exhibitions and demonstrations of Ukrainian folk crafts such as embroidery and ceramics.

Ukrainians in the United States and Canada have created a unique culture within their home countries. This culture has survived discrimination, changed, and grown during the past 130 years. This culture is not just the culture immigrants brought from Ukraine to North America. Ukrainian immigrants adapted their native culture to fit in their adopted countries. This took creativity and perseverance. Over time, Ukrainian culture has become a recognized part of life in North America.

Today, Ukrainian culture is enjoyed not merely by Ukrainians, but also by a countless number of their non-Ukrainian neighbors. This is especially true in western Canada, where Ukrainians make up a high proportion of the population. Ukrainian dance groups, musicians, and choirs perform throughout the world, and Ukrainian festivals are enjoyed by everyone. This is a sign that the cultural contribution of Ukrainians is becoming an accepted part of the multicultural nations of Canada and the United States.

• Study Questions •

1. Why were Ukrainians interned in Canada during World War I?

2. What are fraternal societies, and why were they important to early Ukrainian immigrants?

3. Why were education and newspapers important to Ukrainians in North America?

4. What is the hopak?

7

The Newest Ukrainians in North America

Since the end of World War II in 1945, new waves of Ukrainians have come to the United States and Canada. These newer Ukrainian immigrants shared some things in common with the Ukrainians who had come in the years before and just after World War I. They wanted a better life for their families while preserving their love of Ukrainian heritage. They have also been quite different. Many have been political refugees who did not want to return to Ukraine. Some were well educated and came with a strong love of Ukrainian culture that they developed in Europe rather than in North America.

The new arrivals have had mixed relations with the already-established Ukrainian community: There has been both conflict and cooperation. Ukrainian organizations in the United States and Canada welcomed the newcomers and sometimes lobbied the government to allow more Ukrainians to come to

North America. The newcomers did not always feel comfortable with the existing Ukrainian community, however. Many did not know English and had a hard time communicating with the Ukrainians in North America.

The experiences of the newcomers and existing groups were very different. The new arrivals were going through the hard process of adjustment to a country and had many problems to overcome, just like earlier immigrants did. They often did not have time to repay the older Ukrainian community by taking an active role in community affairs and joining organizations. The existing Ukrainian community viewed this with dismay because they counted on the new arrivals to help build their community and provide "new blood." Some saw the newcomers as aloof, cold, and ungrateful for the help they had received. Some new arrivals from Communist-controlled Ukraine had a strong dislike for joining organizations that they associated with government control.

As time went by, the two groups found more and more common ground. Ukrainians who immigrated after World War II adjusted to life in North America and either joined existing Ukrainian community organizations or formed new groups on their own. Later arrivals in the 1990s had a similar experience and are still in the process of adjusting and finding their place among the Ukrainian communities of North America.

POST–WORLD WAR II IMMIGRANTS

After World War II, the fate of Ukrainian refugees was especially tragic. Many had been taken as slave laborers by the Nazis. They worked for years in the German war industry and for large companies such as Volkswagen. They were horribly mistreated and abused. Some Ukrainian refugees fled the fighting between the Germans and the Soviets that raged in their homeland. Others had no desire to live under Soviet rule again, and a few had actively fought against the Soviet Union in the ranks of the German forces. These refugees were known as displaced persons, or DPs, for short.

At the end of the war, the Soviets demanded the return of all Ukrainians who were in refugee camps in Western Europe, about 2 million people. Most of the Ukrainians refused to go back. In some places, British and American troops forcibly removed the refugees and put them in trucks to be sent back to the Soviet Union. All those who returned were persecuted by the Soviets as "enemies of the Soviet Union." Many were sent to Siberia, and many died.

As the British and Americans began to realize the horror that awaited those who were sent back to the Soviet Union, the forced deportations stopped. This meant that there were about 220,000 Ukrainian refugees who needed to find a place to call home.

Life in the camps was difficult even if it was an improvement over what the prisoners had experienced during the war. Many of the DPs were sick or malnourished because of their mistreatment. The hardest part of being a refugee was the uncertainty—not knowing what would happen to them. They were kept in the camps and could work in the nearby communities but could not leave the area. Until a country was willing to take the DPs in, they had to stay in the camps.

In the camps, however, the Ukrainian DPs had a chance to rebuild their lives. Quite a few of them were educated, and they soon began to organize schools and groups to maintain their language and culture and to make life easier. This became more important as people in the camps began to marry and have children. In the camps, there were 1,500 Ukrainian teachers who organized 70 kindergartens, 102 elementary schools, 30 high schools, 43 trade schools, and 2 universities. Cultural life in the camps thrived. In the first year after the war in the part of Germany occupied by American troops, Ukrainian refugees staged 1,820 plays, 1,315 concerts, and 2,044 lectures. There were 49 choirs and 34 drama groups. Each camp had two or three events staged every week. Refugees who came from poorer backgrounds had a chance to experience cultural activities for the first time.

Between 1945 and 1954, both the United States and Canada opened their doors to the Ukrainian DPs. About 40,000 immigrated to Canada and 85,000 to the United States. They were later joined by Ukrainians who had immigrated to other countries, such as Argentina, and later made their way to North America.

Although they had to start life over again in a new land, they also had a chance to create better lives for themselves. One song written by a Ukrainian immigrant to Canada after the war went as follows: "My Ukrainian song,/Oh, so sweet and strong,/Because my mother taught me/To sing this song./ Ukrainian mother, do you hear,/Though you are here in Canada,/Teach your children your songs,/They'll be happy./America's a sister,/Canada—my mother/Here in Canada it's good/To earn money."[15]

Still, the separation from their homes was difficult. Another song expressed this feeling: "When I had earned a little cash,/ The thought occurred to me,/To return to Ukraine,/But I have no country./For Ukraine has been taken,/by various occupiers,/ So work on in Canada,/You poor immigrant./Because Canada is a free land,/Good, like a mother,/Believe in God, work well,/ And you'll have it all."[16]

The postwar immigrants preferred cities to farms. Although many joined existing Ukrainian centers, they also formed new communities. In Canada, many postwar immigrants chose to settle in cities such as Toronto and Winnipeg rather than on the farms of the western prairies. In the United States, cities such as Cleveland, Detroit, Chicago, Newark, and New York were common destinations.

The new arrivals found whatever jobs they could to begin with, but many gradually worked their way up. Some opened successful businesses. Others had the opportunity to get an education or start a professional career.

Post-World War II Ukrainian immigrants often chose not to live in the country and instead settled in cities such as Cleveland, Chicago, and New York, where they opened small businesses and restaurants. One such Ukrainian restaurant is Veselka, which is located in New York City's East Village and serves such traditional Ukrainian fare as borscht and pierogi.

The new arrivals were much more interested in politics than the first wave of Ukrainians. Because of their experiences in the DP camps, they were also familiar with forming organizations. They were very active in groups that lobbied on behalf of Ukraine's independence and for human rights for Ukrainians. Among the most important groups was the Ukrainian Congress Committee of America (UCCA). During the height of the cold war, the UCCA spoke out against Soviet human rights violations, initiated a U.S. Congressional resolution on the Soviet destruction of Ukrainian churches, supported a U.S. Congressional resolution to commemorate the victims of the 1932–1933 Ukrainian Terror-Famine, and was instrumental in promoting the Captive Nations Week Resolution in 1959. The UCCA was a founding organization of the *National Captive Nations Committee* (NCNC), which united various ethnic organizations with the goal of promoting democracy worldwide. (The Captive Nations program was an effort to raise awareness of the plight of countries that were denied freedom. It encouraged Americans and others to remember those countries and work for democracy and human rights.)

The UCCA's activities created awareness about Ukraine, Ukrainian Americans, and Soviet repression in Ukraine. By supporting organizations such as the NCNC and individuals who stand for freedom of conscience and freedom of speech, as well as by organizing campaigns to free imprisoned dissidents in Ukraine, the UCCA took an active role in Ukraine's struggle for liberation from Communist oppression. Ukrainians worked actively with many other ethnic groups in this effort, putting aside differences for the common goal of freedom.

Immigrants From Soviet Ukraine

From the late 1950s to the 1980s, a small number of Ukrainians arrived in North America. These immigrants came from Soviet-controlled Ukraine or sometimes from Ukrainian minorities in other Communist-dominated countries. Exactly how many came during this period is unknown, because the U.S. and Canadian governments lumped Ukrainians with other citizens of the Soviet Union. About 10,000 went to Canada and more to the United States.

The Ukrainians in this wave were sometimes dissenters who left because of repression by the Soviet government. Many were Jewish, because the Soviet government began to treat its Jewish citizens more harshly after 1968. Some were just ordinary immigrants who managed to win permission to leave to rejoin family who already lived in the West. Most of the Ukrainian immigrants during this period were well-educated professionals. On arriving in North America, these immigrants did not often join existing Ukrainian communities. They followed jobs and education to different parts of North America.

In the 1980s, Soviet power began to weaken and it was increasingly possible for Ukrainians to leave their country. Some were able to go to neighboring countries such as Poland, which threw off Communist rule in 1989. From there, they were able to make their way to Western Europe or North America.

Newcomers From a Free Ukraine

In 1991, as the Soviet Union collapsed, Ukraine achieved independence at long last. Ukrainians in North America were jubilant that their dream of seeing an independent Ukraine had at last come true. A new Ukraine also meant a new wave of immigration. Ukrainians were at last free to travel abroad to work, visit, or reunite their scattered families. Of course, immigrating to Canada or the United States was not always possible because of restrictions on the number of legal immigrants in both countries.

Yet, since 1991, a large number of Ukrainian immigrants have arrived in North America—as many as 200,000 in the United States and 40,000 in Canada. These immigrants came from all parts of Ukraine. Among them were Ukrainian Jews and Poles and ethnic Russians from eastern Ukraine.

This most recent wave of immigrants is made up of many educated professionals, including doctors, professors, scientists, and engineers. More than 70 percent of these Ukrainian immigrants had a degree from a college or a university.

Because they often do not know English well or are unfamiliar with American and Canadian culture, the newest wave of Ukrainians have begun by taking simple jobs. These jobs are often at lower levels than they were used to in Ukraine. For example, a professor might work as a cab driver, a chemist as a construction worker, or an engineer as a home health aide. These jobs allow the new immigrants to pay their bills and save a little money.

Most aspire to raise their status and learn new skills. One example is that many new Ukrainian immigrants are learning computer skills and seeking work with high-tech companies. Others are learning about business with the goal of perhaps starting their own companies.

The new arrivals are not yet joining the existing Ukrainian communities in large numbers. Some are too busy adjusting to life in a new country. Others feel culturally different from Ukrainians who have lived in North America for many years or whose families have been here for generations. The newcomers often prefer to speak Russian rather than Ukrainian, and this also creates some tension with the established Ukrainian communities who conduct their affairs in English or Ukrainian. The new immigrants remain very interested in Ukraine and its culture, however. Through the Internet and telephone, they keep in close contact with friends and family back home in Ukraine and often read Ukrainian newspapers on the Internet.

HELPING UKRAINE

After Ukraine won independence, many Ukrainian Americans and Canadians were eager to assist their newly independent homeland. The transition to democracy and free markets in

Ukraine was very difficult (and continues to be as this book goes to press), and Ukrainian culture and the sense of self-reliance had been damaged by Soviet rule. Use of the Ukrainian language declined because of efforts to make people speak Russian.

Many individual Ukrainians from North America were able to visit their ancestral homeland and renew ties with relatives

JEWISH IMMIGRANTS FROM UKRAINE

Ukraine's Jewish community has an ancient history. The first Jewish travelers came to Ukraine during the period of Kievan Rus (from the late 900s to the mid-1100s), but large-scale Jewish immigration began during the period of Polish-Lithuanian rule (1300 to 1600). During that time, Jews came to central and eastern Europe to escape persecution in other regions of Europe.

Jewish people were welcomed because they brought needed skills. Many were craftsmen, tailors, shoemakers, jewelers, scribes, doctors, and scholars. Others were merchants. They helped develop the economy. In return, Jews were given religious freedom and could govern their own affairs. Jewish communities were protected by the king. Although some people disliked Jews because their religion was different or because they had skills others did not, most of the time Jews and their non-Jewish neighbors got along with each other. In the 1650s, though, there was violence against Jews during Chmielnicki's Uprising, because many peasants started to blame Jews for their poverty.

When the Russian Empire took control of Ukraine in the mid-1600s, the special freedoms Jews had enjoyed were taken away. Both Jews and Christians in Ukraine suffered under the harsh regime. In the 1890s, a new form of prejudice came to Ukraine. Anti-Semitism was a belief that Jews were not just adherents to a different religion, but were members of a different, inferior race. Many in the Russian Empire believed this, and this resulted in violence against Jews in Ukraine. These violent outbursts were known as pogroms.

for the first time. For many, aiding Ukraine first meant helping their relatives avoid poverty. People sent money and packages of clothes and other needed items.

Others used their business and professional ties to help businesses and organizations in Ukraine. North American universities were active in bringing Ukrainian professors and students to Canada and the United States for research and study.

Poverty and the threat of violence encouraged many Jewish people to leave Ukraine and move to North America. These immigrants settled throughout the country, but especially on the East Coast of the United States. They formed large and vibrant communities where they spoke Yiddish (a language that is a mixture of German and Hebrew, as well as Ukrainian and Polish).

During World War II, many Jews who had remained in Ukraine fell victim to the Nazi Holocaust. Many ancient Jewish communities, especially in western and central Ukraine, were destroyed forever. Other Jews survived. Some left Europe and came to North America, and others traveled to the new Jewish state of Israel.

Under Soviet rule, Jews were also mistreated. Many sought to leave and go to Israel or the United States. There was an international campaign on their behalf that convinced the Soviet government to let many emigrate. Other Jews remained and were active in protesting Soviet repression. These people were sometimes called "refuseniks," because they did not want to serve in the Soviet Army.

Since the fall of the Soviet Union in 1991, more Jews have left Ukraine for Israel and North America. At the same time, the Jewish community in Ukraine has slowly begun to revive—many schools, synagogues, and organizations have been created in recent years.

Today, there are 5 to 6 million Jewish Americans and Jewish Canadians. Many of them have roots in Ukraine.

On August 24, 1991, Ukraine won its independence from the Soviet Union, which touched off celebrations in both Ukraine and abroad. Here, Ukrainians celebrate outside the capitol building in Kiev on August 24, which is today celebrated by Ukrainians as a national holiday.

New textbooks and teaching methods in economics and business were translated from English as part of an effort to develop a more modern educational system in Ukraine. This effort was often led by faculty of Ukrainian descent or from other central and eastern European countries who wanted to help Ukraine get back on its feet.

The UCCA redirected its efforts toward supporting Ukraine's democratic development and economic rebirth. The UCCA also began to institute programs to help restore Ukrainians' national consciousness and pride, develop a national education system, and promote the use of the Ukrainian language.

In addition to its continued work in conducting charitable and educational programs, the UCCA began to implement various comprehensive civic education programs, including "get out the vote" preelection campaigns, U.S. study tours for Ukrainian freedom activists and journalist, and "Rock the Vote" youth concerts. UCCA also educates children and students about Ukraine's history and culture by producing audiocassettes and CD-ROMs that are sent free of charge to schools, libraries, and orphanages throughout Ukraine.

One of the most interesting efforts to aid Ukraine occurred in Canada. In 1992, when the Ukrainian government needed to create a new currency system, it did not have the ability to print the money it needed. There was also the problem of possible corruption and counterfeiting. Because of the strong Ukrainian presence in Canada, the Ukrainian government turned to Canada for help. In 1996, the bills of the new Ukrainian currency, the *hryvnia*—printed in Canada—were introduced with great success. This helped the Ukrainian economy take a big step toward independence. Since that time, the National Bank of Ukraine has been able to print its own money. The original bills printed in Canada with the date "1992" (when Ukraine's National Bank was established) will soon become collectors' items!

THE ORANGE REVOLUTION

In 2004, Ukraine held a presidential election to replace outgoing President Leonid Kuchma. During his presidency, Kuchma had become increasingly powerful and had tried to restrict the practice of democracy. Free newspapers and television stations had a hard time surviving because of government interference. The president and many of his associates ran Ukraine like it was a private corporation. Corruption and shady business practices were common, which made it difficult for the Ukrainian economy to recover from Soviet rule. Kuchma's rule made many Ukrainians depressed and apathetic about the future. In addition, the president developed closer and closer links with

Russia, raising fears that Russia might eventually try to gain control of Ukraine and once again extinguish independence.

The election featured two candidates: Viktor Yanukovych and Viktor Yushchenko. Yanukovych was President Kuchma's handpicked candidate. He had the backing of the government, including most of the television stations and newspapers, which were under government control. Yushchenko was the opposition candidate. He vowed to clean up corruption and bring greater democracy to Ukraine. During the campaign, many members of the opposition were attacked or harassed by the government's police and security forces. Yushchenko himself survived a mysterious attempt to assassinate him using poison. The effects of the poison ravaged his face.

On Election Day, November 21, large numbers of Ukrainians turned out to vote. Despite the intimidation by the government, most voted for Yushchenko—but the government secretly tried to change the results to make it look as if Yanukovych had won. When Ukrainians realized this, they staged peaceful, nonviolent protests to demand a new and fair election. Tens of thousands, then hundreds of thousands, of people, young and old, flowed into the streets. The protesters, wearing the orange color of the opposition, paralyzed the government. The world's media began to follow the events in Ukraine.

In Canada and the United States, the dramatic events in Ukraine electrified the Ukrainian community. Almost every community organized demonstrations in support of democracy in Ukraine. New immigrants joined third- and fourth-generation Ukrainian Americans and Canadians in a common goal. They contacted the American media and local elected leaders as well as churches and other ethnic groups. Many raised money to help the protesters.

In December 2004, the government of Ukraine gave in to the protesters and agreed to hold a new election under international supervision. Many Ukrainians from North America traveled

Three Ukrainian-American girls show their support for Ukrainian presidential candidate Viktor Yushchenko at a rally near Rochester, New York, in December 2004. Yushchenko initially lost the 2004 presidential election, but after it was determined that the standing government had committed election fraud, the Ukrainian Supreme Court called for a revote, and Yushchenko was elected on December 26.

to Ukraine to be observers at voting places across Ukraine to ensure that people could vote without fear or corruption. This election had a very different result: Reform candidate Victor Yushchenko won an overwhelming victory.

For Ukrainians in North America, it was a moment of great triumph. Since the first immigrants had arrived from Ukraine, their homeland had never been truly free. Freedom for Ukraine had been a goal for generations. At last they had finally been able to play an important role in helping Ukraine take a big step toward real freedom. For the Ukrainian community, it was a dream come true.

STARTING A NEW CENTURY

More than 125 years have passed since the first large groups of Ukrainian immigrants arrived in North America. An observer who saw these first immigrants might have thought that they had little future in North America. They came without knowing English and with almost no money. Most of the early immigrants had little education; they came with "only their 10 fingers."

With those fingers, they built homes, farms, churches, schools, and businesses. With those fingers, they played music, created sculptures and paintings, composed songs, and wrote books. They found a North America of windswept prairies and smoky industries. With work and ingenuity, they transformed the prairies into fertile farms and turned the factories and coal-mining towns into places of life and song.

The new Ukrainian immigrants who have arrived in recent years will not face as many hardships; nor will they face the discrimination many of the early Ukrainian immigrants experienced. They still must struggle to make themselves at home in North America, however, and they, too, must learn to combine their Ukrainian heritage with the experiences of life in a new country into something unique and lasting.

As the Ukrainian communities in North America begin the new century, many older organizations are gradually losing members. Fraternal insurance societies have experienced a slow decline in membership—yet they remain financially strong and still have much potential. At the same time, new organizations have appeared. There has been a growth of Ukrainian cultural and dance groups in both Canada and the United States. As the latest wave of immigrants finds its place in North America, it will bring new ideas and new vitality to the Ukrainian community.

The future of the Ukrainian community in North America also depends on the future of Ukraine. Ukraine has its freedom, but many serious problems remain. During the Kuchma years, Ukraine fell behind many of the other former Communist-controlled countries that embraced free markets and democracy much sooner. It has a long way to go to catch up. New economic and political reforms are needed. Ukraine also faces environmental problems, some of them a result of the Chernobyl nuclear disaster in 1986.

The United States, Canada, and many European countries, including Poland, are friendly toward Ukraine. Old feelings of resentment between Poles and Ukrainians were put aside when Poles enthusiastically supported the Orange Revolution. Many problems remain between Ukraine and Russia, however. Russia's leaders and many ordinary Russians still feel that Ukraine belongs to Russia, and Russia still has strong influence in many parts of Ukraine. Nevertheless, freedom has provided Ukraine an opportunity for the first time in its history. Today, the Ukrainians have a say in how their country will be run.

For the Ukrainian community of North America, this means a time of change. Older generations of immigrants came from a Ukraine that is very different from the Ukraine of today. They will need to see Ukraine in a new way. It will be less of a place to send help and more of a partner.

Cultural and family ties will remain important to Ukrainian Americans and Canadians, but new relationships are also beginning to form. Many now see Ukraine as a place to do business. There are new ties being established, as immigrants are helping to start businesses in Ukraine or working to build trade with Ukraine. Others are interested in educational and student exchanges with Ukraine that will help educate the next generation of Ukrainian leaders while building cultural understanding.

The values that helped the Ukrainian community survive and thrive in North America—hard work, perseverance, and creativity—will surely be needed as Ukrainian immigrants and their children and grandchildren begin this new era. The Ukrainian immigrants overcame many obstacles in North America, and their descendants have inherited much. New challenges and opportunities await them. As Ukraine grows closer to the United States and Canada, the Ukrainian community of North America will remain an enduring part of all three countries.

• Study Questions •

1. What does "DP" stand for and who are DPs?
....

2. Why did Ukrainians wish to come to North America after World War II?
....

3. How have Ukrainians in North America assisted Ukraine?
....

4. How did Ukrainians in North America feel about the Orange Revolution?
....

Chronology

1600s–1700s   Early Ukrainian pioneers may have come to America as early as the 1600s; in the 1700s, some Ukrainians served in the American Revolutionary War.

1784   The first Russian outpost is established in Alaska; among the early settlers are Ukrainian Cossacks.

1812   The Russian colony at Fort Ross, near present-day San Francisco, is established, with many Ukrainians participating in its founding.

1814   Taras Shevchenko, the national poet of Ukraine, is born.

1868   Father Agapius Honcharenko, a Ukrainian priest, writer, and translator, establishes the bilingual paper the *Alaska Herald*, one of the new American territory's first newspapers.

1870s   Small groups of Ukrainian immigrants from Austria-Hungary begin to arrive in America.

1885   The first Ukrainian church in North America, St. Michael the Archangel In Shenandoah, Pennsylvania, is completed.

1886   Father Ivan Wolansky founds *Amerika*, the world's first Ukrainian newspaper, in Shenandoah, Pennsylvania.

1887   The first Ukrainian-American choir is founded in Shenandoah, Pennsylvania.

1890   The first group of Ukrainian Protestant immigrants arrives in the United States; they eventually settle on farms in North Dakota.

1891   Wasyl Eleniak and Ivan Pylypiw arrive in Canada as the first permanent Ukrainian settlers in that country; Father Alexis Toth converts to the Russian Orthodox Church after a dispute with the bishop of St. Paul, Minnesota; Father Toth actively works to convert other Ukrainian immigrants to the Russian Church.

1892   The Union of Greek Catholic Brotherhoods in North America is founded as the first national fraternal organization for Ukrainians and Carpatho-Rusyns.

1893   The first Ukrainian school in North America is established in Pennsylvania.

1894   The Ukrainian National Association is founded in Shamokin, Pennsylvania; UNA later becomes the largest Ukrainian organization in North America.

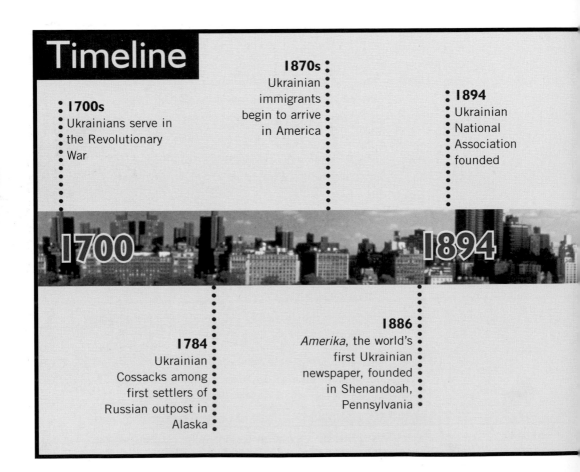

Timeline

1700s
Ukrainians serve in the Revolutionary War

1870s
Ukrainian immigrants begin to arrive in America

1894
Ukrainian National Association founded

1700   **1894**

1784
Ukrainian Cossacks among first settlers of Russian outpost in Alaska

1886
Amerika, the world's first Ukrainian newspaper, founded in Shenandoah, Pennsylvania

1897   The Sisterhood of St. Olga, the first Ukrainian women's organization in North America, is founded in Jersey City, New Jersey.

1907   Soter Stephen Ortynsky is appointed as the first Ukrainian Catholic bishop in North America.

1913   The Ukrainian Catholic exarchate is established in North America with more than 200 parishes.

1918   Efforts to establish an independent Ukraine begin in Kiev and other cities.

1920   The Soviet Union extinguishes efforts to form an independent Ukraine; after this, about 40,000 Ukrainian immigrants come to the United States and another 70,000 to Canada.

1924   The first Ukrainian theater in the United States is founded.

1950s
Many Ukrainians immigrate to North America

1907
Soter Stephen Ortynsky becomes first Ukrainian Catholic bishop in North America

2004
The "Orange Revolution" occurs in Ukraine

1907

2004

1991
Ukraine declares independence

1932
Terror-Famine in Ukraine begins

1930   The first Ukrainian radio program is broadcast in North America.

1932   The Soviet Terror-Famine in Ukraine begins.

1939   Ukrainian immigrant Igor Sikorsky pioneers the first successful helicopter in America; World War II begins in Europe—Canada enters the war on the side of the Allies, and many Ukrainian Canadians serve in the armed forces.

1941   Ukraine falls under the rule of Nazi Germany; the United States enters World War II—many Ukrainian Americans serve in the armed forces.

1945   World War II ends.

1950   Jack Palance makes his movie debut in *Panic in the Streets*.

1950s   Many new Ukrainian immigrants come to the United States and Canada.

1986   Disaster occurs at the Chernobyl nuclear power plant in Ukraine.

1991   The Soviet Union collapses, and Ukraine declares independence.

2004   The "Orange Revolution" occurs in Ukraine.

Notes

Chapter 3

1. Anthony J. Amato, *In the Wild Mountains: Idiom, Economy, and Ideology among the Hutsuls, 1849 to 1939*, Ph.D. diss. Department of History (Bloomington: Indiana University, 1998), 230–65.
2. "N.D. Marks 100 Years of Ukrainian settlement," *Ukrainian Weekly*, July 21, 1996, available online at *http://www.ukrweekly.com/Archive/1996/299616.shtml*
3. Ibid.
4. Ibid.
5. Ibid.
6. "Steerage Conditions," Reports of the U.S. Immigration Commission, 61st Cong., 3rd sess. Washington, D.C.: Government Printing Office, 1911.

Chapter 4

7. Myrna Kostash, *All of Baba's Children* (Edmonton, Alberta, Canada: NeWest Press, 1992), 13. Reprint of 1977 edition.
8. Ibid., 14.

9. Quoted in Myron B. Kuropas, *Ukrainian Citadel: The First One Hundred Years of the Ukrainian National Association* (Boulder, Colo.: East European Monographs, 1996), 31.

Chapter 5

10. Kostash, *All of Baba's Children*, 177.
11. Ibid., 178.
12. Ibid., 115.
13. Ibid., 122.

Chapter 6

14. Quote from the *Vegreville Observer*, July 28, 1908, in Kostash, *All of Baba's Children*, 32.

Chapter 7

15. Thomas M. Prymak, "Ukrainian DP Folklore: A Neglected Legacy," *Ukrainian Weekly*, April 18, 2004, available online at *http://www.ukrweekly.com/Archive/2004/160423.shtml*
16. Ibid.

Glossary

babka   A sweet bread often eaten around Easter time.

borscht   Beet soup.

Carpatho-Rusyns   Mountaineers who live in western Ukraine, southern Poland, and Slovakia who are very closely related to Ukrainians; sometimes called "Ruthenians."

Chernobyl   A Soviet nuclear plant and the site of the world's worst nuclear accident in 1986.

Cossacks   A brotherhood of free warriors established to guard the southern border of the Polish-Lithuanian Commonwealth. Many Ukrainians view the Cossacks as the forefathers of modern Ukrainians.

displaced persons (DPs)   A term for refugees after World War II.

Donbas   The basin of the River Don, the industrial and mining region of eastern Ukraine.

Ellis Island   The U.S. immigration station in New York, where many Ukrainian immigrants first arrived in America.

fraternal insurance   A type of inexpensive insurance developed by many immigrants, including Ukrainians.

Galicia   A region of southeastern Poland and western Ukraine from which many Ukrainians came.

Holodomor   The Ukrainian word for the Terror-Famine in the 1930s, when Ukraine's Soviet rulers deliberately starved millions of people to death.

hopak   A type of Ukrainian folk dance.

hryvnia   The currency of independent Ukraine.

Kievan Rus   The first Ukrainian kingdom, which existed from the 900s to the 1200s.

kokhanochka   A type of Ukrainian folk dance.

kolachi   A pastry.

kovbasa   Ukrainian sausage.

kutia   Christmas wheat porridge mixed with poppy seeds and honey.

National Captive Nations Committee   A group formed by ethnic groups whose homelands were invaded by the Soviet Union.

Orange Revolution   A peaceful movement to secure Ukrainian independence that occurred in 2004 and 2005.

pashka   A type of Ukrainian bread eaten at Easter.

pysanky   Colored Ukrainian Easter eggs.

Slavic   A large ethnic and language group that lives in eastern, central, and southern Europe. Ukrainians are one of many Slavic peoples.

Stundists   A Ukrainian Protestant group.

Ukrainian National Association (UNA)   The oldest and largest Ukrainian-American organization.

varenyky   Dumplings filled with cheese or other fillings; better known as pierogi.

Bibliography

Halich, Wasyl. *Ukrainians in the United States.* New York: Arno Press and the *New York Times,* 1970.

Isajiw, Wsevolod W., Yury Boshyk, and Roman Senkus, eds. *The Refugee Experience: Ukrainian Displaced Persons after World War II.* Toronto: Canadian Institute of Ukrainian Studies Press, 2004.

Kostash, Myrna. *All of Baba's Children.* Edmonton, Alberta, Canada: NeWest Press, 1992.

Kuropas, Myron. *The Ukrainian Americans: Roots and Aspirations.* Toronto: University of Toronto Press, 1991.

——. *Ukrainian-American Citadel: The First One Hundred Years of the Ukrainian National Association.* New York: EEM/Columbia University Press, 1997.

Osborn, Kevin. *The Ukrainian Americans.* New York: Chelsea House, 1989.

Subtelny, Orest. *Ukraine: A History,* 2nd ed. Toronto: University of Toronto Press, 1994.

Wertsman, Vladimir. *The Ukrainians in America, 1608–1975.* Dobbs Ferry, N.Y.: Oceana Publishers, 1976.

Woloch Vaughn, Mary Ann. *Ukrainian Christmas: Traditions, Folk Customs, and Recipes.* New York: Ukrainian Heritage Co., 1983.

——. *Ukrainian Easter: Traditions, Folk Customs, and Recipes.* New York: Communications Print, 1982.

Further Reading

BOOKS

Kostash, Myrna. *All of Baba's Children.* Edmonton, Alberta, Canada: NeWest Press, 1992.

Osborn, Kevin. *The Ukrainian Americans.* New York: Chelsea House, 1989.

WEB SITES

Ukrainian Bandurist Chorus
www.bandura.org

Ukrainian Displaced Persons
www.brama.com/news/press/030311subtelny_DPcamps.html

John Radzilowski, "Ukraine: Freedom Cannot Be Stopped"
www.frontpagemag.com/Articles/ReadArticle.asp?ID=16193

Internment of Ukrainians in Canada, 1914–1920
www.infoukes.com/history/internment/

Ukrainian Museum of New York
www.ukrainianmuseum.org/index.html

Ukrainian Weekly
www.ukrweekly.com

Vesnivka Chorus
www.vesnivka.com/

Picture Credits

Index

A

Alaska
  native rights, 13
  purchase of, 12
  Ukrainian communities in, 55
Alaska Herald (newspaper), 13, 87
American Civil War
  Ukrainian soldiers, 12
American Revolutionary War, 12
Amerika (newspaper), 87
Archipenko, Alexander
  painting and sculpting, 16
Argentina
  Ukrainian communities in,
    51, 97
arts and sciences, 15
  architecture, 18
  folk crafts, 92
  music and dance, 20, 26, 76,
    88–93, 97, 108–109
  painting, 16, 20, 108
  sculpting, 16, 108
  theater, 88–89
Asia
  ancient, 22
Australia
  Ukrainian communities in, 51
Austria-Hungary
  immigrants, 13, 53
  rule of Ukraine, 13–15, 26–27,
    77, 82–83

B

Babi Yar, 32
Bandurists, 91
Banff National Park, 83

Basaraba, Pearl, 43
Basaraba, Peter, 42
Battle of Blue Waters, 24
Batu Khan, 23
Belarus, 21
Black Sea, 21–22
Bondar, Roberta, 16
Bremen, Germany
  port city, 44
business, 63
  boardinghouse, 61
  food service and industry, 62
  saloons, 60–61
  seamstress, 61
Byzantine Empire, 23

C

Canada
  cities, 11
  culture, 89, 101
  economy, 49
  famous immigrants, 16–18
  farming in, 55, 57–58, 62–63,
    80
  future, 20
  government, 49, 82–83, 94, 100,
    105, 109
  history, 62, 88
  military, 83
  multicultural nation, 12
Captive Nations Week Resolution,
  99
Carpathian Mountains, 13, 76–77
Carpatho-Rusyns (Ruthenians), 22
  immigration, 13, 50, 76
Catholic, Ukrainian

American bishops, 78
divisions, 76–79
early, 24–26, 77
persecution, 28, 32
tradition, 69
Chernobyl nuclear power plant
disaster at, 34, 109
Chicago
Ukrainian communities in, 54,
63, 97
Chickamauga, Battle of, 12
Chmielnicki's Uprising, 102
Christianity, 102
early, 23
traditions, 66, 69, 90
Christmas
caroling, 38–40, 65, 67, 71
date of, 66
food, 70
traditions, 65, 69–70
churches, 15, 99
divided traditions, 74, 76–80
early, 71–74, 84, 108
and fraternal societies, 56,
84–86
fundraisers, 67
publications, 88
rituals and holidays, 38, 40,
67–71, 84
sense of identity, 71–74, 87, 89
Coal and Iron Police, 57
coal mining
communities, 14–15, 20, 42–43,
53–57, 60–65, 71
dangers of, 55–57, 81, 84–85
illnesses and injuries from, 56
treatment of workers, 56
unions, 57
cold war, 99
Communism, 88, 99
revolutionaries, 27–28
in Ukraine, 34–35, 95, 100, 109
communities, 15, 28
early, 60, 64, 70–72, 80, 95
making of, 81, 84–89, 108–109
and new arrivals, 94–110

rural, 11–12, 14, 20, 53–59,
63, 71
urban, 11–12, 14, 20, 58, 60,
62–63, 74, 97
Constantinople, Turkey, 79
Cossacks, Ukrainian
rebellion, 25
Crimean Peninsula
attacks on, 28, 30–32
early settlements on, 21–22,
25
desire for better life, 18–19, 27,
32, 41–42, 47, 53, 63–64, 94
holidays, 64–71
love of homeland, 19–20, 94,
97, 110
promotion and preservation of,
56, 63, 65–66, 78, 81, 85–94,
96, 101, 105, 109
and secret societies, 26–27
spiritual, 38, 64
and traditions, 64–66, 71, 74,
76
Cyprus
Ukrainian communities in, 51
Cyrillic lettering, 11
Czechoslovakia, 22
Ukrainian communities in, 28

D

discrimination, 15
in Canada, 81–83, 92
in Europe, 28
in United States, 81–82, 92
Dmytruk, Natalia, 35
Dnieper River, 23

E

Easter
egg coloring (pysanky), 66,
68–69
foods, 65, 68–69
Good Friday, 69
Lent, 68

Palm Sunday, 68
  traditions, 65, 68–69
education, 15
  denial of, 62, 82, 108
  improvements in, 62–63, 76,
    87, 96–97, 100–101, 104–
    105, 110
  promotion of, 88
Eleniak, Wasyl
  settles in Canada, 14
Ellis Island
  arrival to, 45, 47
  closing, 47
Europe
  ancient, 22–23, 26
  countries, 21, 50–51, 104, 109
  immigration, 44–45, 50–51, 55,
    61, 82, 102–103
  war and devastation in, 14, 30,
    32
European Union, 51

F

farming, 12, 20, 108
  in Canada, 55, 57–58, 62–63, 80
  on the Great Plains, 15, 57–60,
    80
  hardships, 58–60, 64–65
  land for, 58
Feast of St. Nicholas. *See* Christmas
festivals and rituals
  blessing of water, 38
  Christmas, 65–67, 69–71
  Easter, 65–69
  and societies, 84, 89, 92–93
food, favorite, 20, 62, 89, 92
  babka, 11–12
  borscht, 71–73
  holubtsi, 71
  kolachi, 11, 70
  kovbasa, 11, 69
  kutia, 71
  pashka, 65, 68–69
  uzvar, 71
  varenyky, 11, 71

vushka, 71
Franko, Ivan, 27, 62
fraternal organizations, 15
  insurance, 84–86, 109
  and new immigrants, 94–95,
    99
  promotion of Ukrainian
    culture, 56, 81, 85–86, 88,
    92–93

G

George V, King of England, 83
Germany
  armies, 29, 32, 96
  refugee camps in, 46, 95–96
  Ukrainian communities in,
    28–32
Golden Horde, 23–24
Great Britain
  government, 82–83
  military, 46, 96
Greece
  ancient, 22
  religion, 76

H

Hamburg, Germany
  port city, 43–44
Hawaii
  Ukrainian communities in,
    55
Hitler, Adolf
  and World War II, 28–29
Hnatyshyn, Ramon,
  politics, 16–17
Holocaust, 32, 103
Honcharenko Agapius
  Alaska Herald, 13, 87
  criticism of Russian emperor,
    12
  occupations, 12–13
Hopak, 88
Hruby, Mary Skoropat, 42
Humeniuk, Pawlo, 90

Hungary
kingdom, 77
religion, 76

I

immigration hardships
air travel, 47
criminals, 44–45
finding their way, 49–52
language barriers, 44, 49–51,
64, 81, 95, 108
leaving home, 43
loneliness, 64, 97
sea journey, 43–44, 47
train, 43–44
visas and restrictions, 47, 49,
100
immigration statistics
early, 14–15, 43–45, 49–50,
71–74, 76–78, 95, 99, 108
from 1954–1991, 14, 99
after Russian Revolution, 14,
27
today, 15, 47, 49–52, 94, 100–
101, 108–110
Ukrainian ancestry, 12
after Ukrainian independence,
14–15, 34, 101–105
after World War I, 14, 27, 45, 94
after World War II, 14, 32,
45–47, 94–99
internment (1914–1920)
events of, 82–83
Ireland, John, 78
Italy
Ukrainian communities in, 51

J

Judaism
immigration, 102–103
persecution, 25, 28, 30–32, 100,
102–103
in Ukraine, 22, 25–26, 38, 100,
102–103

K

Khmelnytsky, Bohdan
rebellion, 25
Kiev, 47
attacks of, 23, 29
capital, 21, 23
Kievan Rus, 23
Klym, George, 43
Konowal, Philip, 83
Kravchuk, Leonid, 91
Kuchma, Leonid
government of, 35, 105–106,
109
Kumpanii, 39

L

languages
English, 13, 15, 61–62, 81,
87–88, 95, 101, 104, 108
Russian, 13, 22, 26, 28, 34, 50,
79, 101–102
Ukrainian, 22, 26, 28, 34, 50,
57, 61, 71, 74, 76, 78, 87–88,
96, 101–102, 104
Yiddish, 103
Lattimer Massacre, 57
Lenin, V.I., 27
death, 28
Liberia
Ukrainian communities in, 51
literature, Ukrainian, 13, 74
newspaper, 13, 60, 76, 87–88,
101
writers, 26–27, 62, 76, 87–88,
108
Lithuanian
rule of Ukraine, 24–25, 102
Lviv, 24, 32, 43

M

Michigan
Ukrainian communities in,
54–55, 63, 89, 92, 97
Minnesota

Ukrainian communities in, 55,
78–79
Montreal Ukrainian Festival, 89

Orthodox Church
early, 24–25, 76, 79
traditions, 69, 78, 90

N

National Bank of Ukraine, 105
National Captive Nations
Committee (NCNC), 99
Nazi Germany
rule of Ukraine, 29–32, 46
war criminals, 17
and World War II, 28–32, 103
NCNC. *See* National Captive
Nations Committee
New Jersey
Ukrainian communities in,
54, 97
New York
Ukrainian communities in, 54,
63, 97
New Zealand
Ukrainian communities in, 51
Nixon, Richard, 91
North Dakota
farming in, 57–60
Ukrainian communities in, 51,
57–60

O

occupations
businesses, 12, 15, 60–63, 97,
101, 108
farming, 12, 15, 20, 41, 57–60,
62–65, 80, 108
mines and factories, 14–15, 20,
42–43, 53–57, 59–65, 71, 81,
84–85, 91, 108
new wave, 62–63
temporary, 14, 63
Ohio
Ukrainian communities in,
54–55, 63, 97
Orange Revolution
events of, 34–35, 105–109

P

Palance, Jack (Vladimir Palahniuk),
91
actor, 17
City Slickers, 17
Panic in the Streets, 17
Shane, 17
Sudden Fear, 17
Pennsylvania
coal mining in, 43, 54–57, 63
Ukrainian settlements in, 12,
43, 53–57
People of Ukraine, 21
around the world, 49–52
droughts, floods and sickness,
40
family life, 37–41, 58, 65–66,
68, 74, 80, 110
immigration reasons, 37, 41–49
language, 22
peasants, 25, 37–38, 40–42, 50,
63, 71, 74
refugees, 46–47, 91, 94–97, 99
treatment of, 25–26, 30, 46–47,
95–96
village life, 37–41, 44, 74
Peter the Great, 26
Picasso, Pablo, 16
Poland, 53, 109
borders, 21
culture, 76
independence, 27, 34, 100
invasion, 28
massacres, 25, 30–32
people, 22
religion, 76
rule of Ukraine, 24–26, 28,
102
Ukrainian communities in, 28,
50, 100
Poltava, Battle of, 26

Protestant (Stundists)
immigrants, 79–80
Pylypiw, Ivan
settles in Canada, 14

R

railroad companies, 58
Reagan, Ronald, 91
Roman Catholic Church, 76
Romania
borders, 21
Russia, 32, 34, 82
armies, 26
borders, 21
culture, 79
government, 80, 106, 109
rule of Ukraine, 12, 14–15,
25–27, 50, 102
Ukrainian communities in, 50,
100
Russian Orthodox Church
founding, 78–79
and Toth, 78–79
Russian Revolution, 14
Ruthenians. *See* Carpatho-Rusyns

S

Sawchuk, Terry
hockey, 17–18
Scandinavia
Viking troops, 22–23
Scythian Empire, 22
serfdom system, 41
Sheptytsky, Andrei, 32
Shevchenko, Taras
birth, 26
poetry, 26–27, 62
Shore, Dinah, 90
Siberia
exiles to, 28, 32, 47, 50, 96
Slavic tribes
in Ukraine, 22–23
Slovak
culture, 76

Soviet Terror-Famine
victims of, 28, 30–31, 99
Soviet Union
armies, 30
collapse of, 31, 34, 100, 103
government, 27–31, 34, 45–47,
91, 99–100
rule of Ukraine, 20, 28, 30–32,
34, 45–47, 91, 95–96, 99–
100, 102–103, 105
Spain
Ukrainian communities in, 51
sports
hockey, 17–18
Stalin, Joseph
death, 32
and the Soviet Union, 28, 30,
32
Statue of Liberty, 45
Svoboda (newspaper), 87
Sweden, 26

T

Tatars, 22, 25
Teron, William
architecture, 18
Toth, Alexis
converts, 78–79
and the Russian Orthodox
Church, 78–79
Turchin, John Basil (Ivan Vasilevitch
Turchininoff)
and the Civil War, 12

U

UCCA. *See* Ukrainian Congress
Committee of America
Ukraine
early history, 22–23
economy, 35, 37, 50, 55, 63,
102, 104–105, 109
extremists, 30, 32
foreign aid to, 101–105, 109
foreign reign of, 12–15, 19,

24–32, 34, 45–47, 50, 82–83, 91, 95–96, 99–100, 102–103, 105
future, 20, 63, 109
government, 41, 45, 78–79, 94–95, 101, 104–106, 108–109
history, 62, 74, 76, 80, 87, 89, 91, 105
independence, 12, 14–15, 19–20, 34–35, 62–63, 100–101, 104–106, 108
independence attempts, 25–28, 30, 34, 99
land and people, 21–22, 25–26, 30
location, 21
natural resources, 21, 27–28
protests, 35, 106
Terror-Famine in, 28, 30–31, 99
Ukrainian Autocephalos Orthodox Church
founding, 79
Ukrainian Congress Committee of America (UCCA)
activities, 99, 104–105
Ukrainian Museum, 86
Ukrainian National Association (UNA)
branches, 86
founded, 56, 85
newspapers, 87
publications, 87–88
Ukrainian National Women's League of America (UNWLA)
founding, 86
Ukrainian Sunflower Festival, 89, 92
Ukrainian Weekly (newspaper), 87
Ukrainian Youth League of North America, 86
UNA. See Ukrainian National Association

Union Army, 12
United Nations
aid to Ukrainians, 47
United States
cities, 11
culture, 89–90, 101
economy, 55
famous immigrants, 16–18
future, 20
government, 13, 45, 49, 57, 94, 99–100, 109
history, 62, 87–88
military, 46, 96
multicultural nation, 12

V

Veselka (magazine), 88
Vesnivka, 90
Vladimir I, 23

W

Wells, Carveth, 31
Wolansky, Ivan
Amerika, 87
women's organizations, 86
World War I, 14
aftermath, 27, 94
events of, 82
immigration after, 45
World War II, 16
aftermath, 32, 45, 89, 94–99
events of, 28–32, 88, 103
immigration after, 14, 46–47

Y

Yanukovych, Viktor, 106
Yaroslav the Wise, 23
Yushchenko, Victor, 35, 106, 108

About the Contributors

Series Editor **Robert D. Johnston** is associate professor and director of the Teaching of History Program in the Department of History at the University of Illinois at Chicago. He is the author of *The Making of America: The History of the United States from 1492 to the Present*, a middle-school textbook that received a *School Library Journal* Best Book of the Year award. He is currently working on a history of vaccine controversies in American history, to be published by Oxford University Press.

John Radzilowski is an author and historian and is adjunct professor of history at the University of St. Thomas in St. Paul, Minnesota. He has written numerous books and articles on immigration from eastern and central Europe to North America.